TIMOTHY V. RASINSKI & MELISSA CHEESMAN SMITH

DAILY Word Ladders

Content Areas
Grades 4–6

*90 Word Ladders to Boost Word Study Skills and Reinforce Key Concepts in Math, Science, **and More!***

Photos by Kelly Kennedy for Scholastic Inc.

1 2 3 4 5 6 7 8 9 10   40   28 27 26 25 24 23 22 21 20 19

Text pages printed on 10% PCW recycled paper.

Scholastic Inc., 557 Broadway, New York, NY 10012

SCHOLASTIC

CONTENTS

Social Studies Ladders

Science Ladders

Technology Ladders

INTRODUCTION

This book offers you and your students 90 short word study lessons called *word ladders*. To "climb" a word ladder, students make a series of words, progressing from rung to rung up the ladder. At each rung, they follow clues to build a new word from the previous word. Along the way, you take instructional opportunities to help students tackle challenging words as well as to notice the meanings and structures of words—these are teachable moments that support students in building vocabulary, spelling, phonics, and other word study skills, as well as reading comprehension and writing.

In *Daily Word Ladders: Content Areas*, students get bonus word work in language arts, math, science, and social studies—and a fun puzzle to solve with each ladder: The words at the top and bottom of each ladder are connected, and students use those words to complete a sentence at the bottom of the page. The words and sentences reinforce key ideas in the given content area.

We're excited to give you the word ladders you've always loved in an easier-to-navigate format: the ladder page you'll copy for students, along with a new feature: the facing companion Answer Key and Teaching Notes page.

Students' Page   Teacher's Page

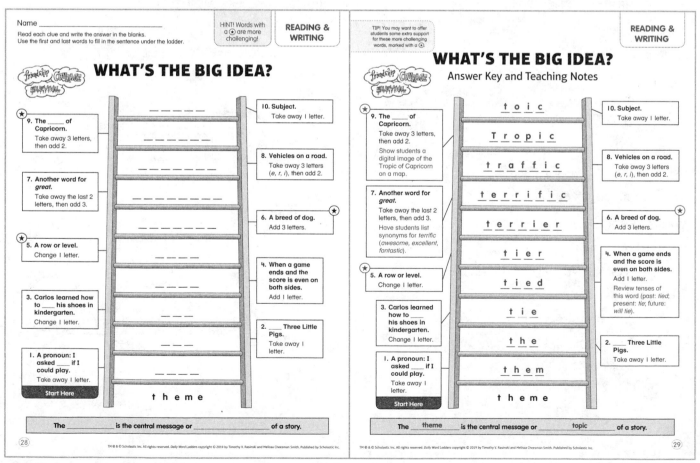

Word Ladders Are Serious Fun

Although word ladders are playful in nature, they also integrate important language learning. For example, as we encourage students to look for meaning first by solving semantic clues for each word (e.g., for *race*, the clue is "a competition"), we help solidify and expand students' comprehension of words and concepts while building vocabulary. And when we ask students to make one word from another by modifying its structure, we are really asking them to examine closely the sound-symbol relationship that exists in the first word in order to determine what changes are required to make the second word—checking all along that the answers make sense. This deep examination of words is just the kind of analysis that all students need to do in order to become both more familiar and fluent with decoding, spelling, and visually recognizing words.

The word ladders in this collection integrate comprehension, vocabulary development, word solving, phonics, and spelling—all key to students' success in learning to read.

WHY CONTENT-AREA WORD LADDERS?

Content-area learning is highly dependent on knowledge of the specialized words, or academic vocabulary, within each content area. Students must, therefore, be able to recognize and understand the key words (and concepts that the words represent) that are integral to those content or subject areas. Providing them with frequent and varied encounters with academic words found in content-area texts, such as *meter* and *president*, builds a foundation for success across subjects.

To this end, the word ladder lessons in this collection should be scheduled routinely to expand students' general and specialized knowledge of words and how words work. Content-area word ladders might also be used as an introduction or follow-up to a specific concept or as an introductory lesson to particular units of study (e.g., folktales, measurement, or branches of government). They can even be used as a daily introductory activity to initiate discussion on a variety of content-related issues. We trust you'll find many ways to weave content-area word ladders into your plans.

Note: In addition to words for math, science, and social studies, we have also included word ladders for technology. These bonus word ladders will allow you to start informative discussions about the technologies we use in our daily lives—fun with words, but with a focus on learning, too!

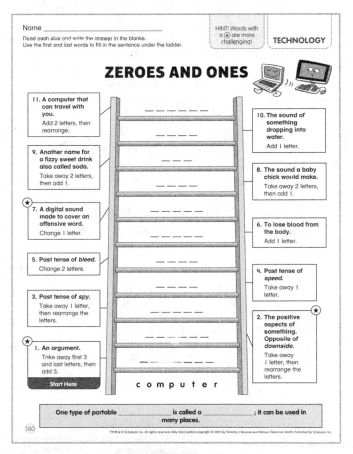

Technology-focused ladders can build background knowledge and technological literacy.

How to Teach a Word Ladder Lesson

Word ladders are very easy to implement and quick to do. Here are some steps to follow:

GETTING STARTED

1. Choose a word ladder lesson related to content students may have recently learned or that you might want to introduce in advance of a unit or lesson.

2. Make a copy of the companion student page for every student in your class and/or project the page on a screen.

3. Go over the steps in the next section with students, as needed. You may also want to make copies of Climb a Word Ladder! for each student, or hang an enlarged copy for reference.

WORKING THROUGH A LADDER WITH STUDENTS

1. **Start at the Bottom:** The first word is given, so students start at the bottom of the ladder and work their way up by reading the next set of clues. In each answer space, the number of blank lines shows the number of letters required for each word and serves as an additional guide for students.

2. **Focus on the First Word:** Before students begin solving the clues, take a moment to discuss the meaning and structure of the initial word with students.

3. **Use Clues to Move Through the Word Ladder:** For every subsequent word, students are given a pair of clues to figure out the word:

   - Semantic Clue: a brief definition or a close-style sentence that includes the word in a meaningful context

   - Letter Clue: the changes required in the previous word in order to make the new word (how many letters to add, drop, or change)

We also encourage you to add your own clues related to a relevant lesson or background knowledge students may have. The more connections you can help students make to previous learning or personal experiences, the better!

4. **Use Teaching Notes to Enhance the Learning:** On your Answer Key and Teaching Notes page, look for instructional notes. These are opportunities to expand students' word study and content knowledge in areas such as

   - synonyms/antonyms

   - parts of speech/tenses of verbs

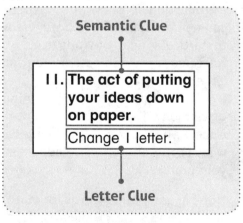

Semantic Clue

11. The act of putting your ideas down on paper.

Change 1 letter.

Letter Clue

Clues for the word *write*.

- homophones/homographs

- syllabication

- rhyming words/spelling patterns

- word categories and associations

- definitions/further explanation of the meaning

- multiple-meaning words

- visual associations (graphics and images)

5. **Assist With Challenging Vocabulary:** "Challenge words" that students may be unfamiliar with are marked with a ⊛ and can be opportunities to develop new vocabulary. Of course, we encourage you to focus on any words you think may be unfamiliar to students by exploring, repeating, and defining those words in context with explanations.

6. **Connect the Words:** When you come to the final word in the lesson, remind students that the <u>last</u> word is connected to the <u>first</u> word on the ladder; they should check their answers by completing the "Mystery Sentence" at the bottom using those two words. If the sentence makes sense, the ladder is likely correct!

7. **Discuss the Title and Illustration for Each Lesson:** To help students expand their content-area understanding, engage them in a discussion about how the title and illustration relate to the key words.

8. **Extend!:** Once the lesson is complete, you may wish to extend the lesson with the extension ideas on the next page.

VARIATIONS

These ideas come straight from Melissa's classroom, where word ladders are a daily favorite! With each idea, make sure to check for students' understanding and review their answers.

> 2. **What you wash dishes in.**
>
> Change 1 letter.
>
> Multiple meaning word: to fall or drop slowly, often in water.

This teaching note expands students' understanding of the word *sink*.

> 5. **A practical joke**
>
> Add 1 letter.

Prank may be a "challenge word" for some students.

WAYS TO PROVIDE EXTRA SUPPORT

Create an Answer Bank: Display all the answers for the ladder in random order on a chart or board. Have children choose words from the list to complete the ladder.

Spell the Words Aloud: After students have figured out a word or made their best guesses, say and spell the answer aloud to allow students the opportunity to double check their own spelling of the word and fix mistakes.

Bring the Words Home: Encourage students to take their completed word ladder home, and challenge family members by reading aloud the clues and asking them to figure out the words.

- **Student Leader:** Invite students to read the clues aloud as you move up the ladder (you might hand out the page in advance of the lesson so students can practice reading). Select students who have their hands up and are ready to give an answer.

- **Snake Around:** Ensure every student is involved by having one student read the first clue aloud and then call on a classmate to answer. The next student in order reads the second clue aloud, calls on a new classmate to answer, and so on. You can keep moving through the seating order over several days with several ladders, so that every student has a chance to read a clue and give an answer.

- **Stand Up!:** Choose one student to stand and read the first clue and call on another student to stand and state the answer. Continue the routine, calling on students who haven't yet had a chance to participate.

EXTENSIONS

- Challenge students to come up with alternative definitions for words that have multiple meanings.

- Add new or interesting words to the classroom word wall from completed ladders. Encourage students to use the words in their speaking and writing (e.g., using the words in written sentences).

- Have students sort the answers from a completed ladder into various categories that you may provide, or categories students come up with based on the set of words. You might focus on **word structure** sorts, such as consonant blend/no consonant blend, number of syllables, long vowels/short vowels, and compound words/non-compound words. **Word meaning** sorts might include parts of speech, positive connotation/negative connotation, one meaning/multiple meanings.

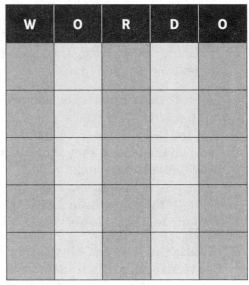

WORDO directions and game cards are available at scholastic.com/DWLresources.

- Play WORDO, which is like BINGO with words instead of numbers. Have students fill in blank WORDO cards in a random order using a bank of words from one or more completed word ladder lesson. To play, you call out the word or a clue to a word, and students find and cover the correct word with a chip or marker. When a student gets five words in a row, column, or diagonal line, he or she may win by calling out "WORDO" first.

- Invite students to make their own word ladders: Give students a first and last word for the ladder that are related to a topic you're studying, current events, or interesting uses of language, such as idioms (e.g., *beat* and *bush* from "Don't beat around the bush"). Then challenge them to make their own word ladders, including clues, that go from the first word to the last word, and then have them trade with a partner to complete each other's ladders. See pages 191–192 for directions for creating a word ladder and page 193 for a word ladder template (also available online).

That's all there is to doing word ladder lessons! They are simple lessons, but the active guidance, engagement, and challenge you provide, whether in a whole class, small group, or individually, will

CLIMB A WORD LADDER!

5. When you've solved all of the clues, use the top word and the bottom word to fill in the mystery sentence at the bottom of the ladder.

4. Keep moving up the ladder until you reach the top!

3. Move up to the next ladder rung. Use the next clue to make a new word.

2. Use the clues to change the first word into a new word that fits in the blanks.

1. Start at the...

3. The player took a ___ on the bench.
Change 1 letter.

4. Direction opposite of west.
Rearrange the letters.

2. To burn at a very high temperature.
Take away the i and rearrange the letters.

1. To take a turn, ___ your hand.
Add 1 letter.

Start Here

e a s t

s e a t

s e a r

r a i s e

r i s e

Hmmm... I think you would raise your hand. If I add one letter, *a*, I can make *raise* from *rise*—it works!

TIP!
Each clue gives you hints about
• the new word's meaning.
• how to change the letters in the last word to make a new one.

BUILD YOUR OWN LADDER!

Materials

Use **two copies** of a blank word ladder template (page 193 or online).

• **Copy 1:** This is your answer key!
• **Copy 2:** This copy is for your friends to solve!

Directions

1. Choose two related words that aren't too long. Examples:
   • *big-large* (synonyms)
   • *sum-add* (topics you're studying)
   • *field-day* (events/news)

2. On Copy 1, write one word at the top of your ladder and one word at the bottom of your ladder.

3. List all the words in between, changing a letter or two at a time with each new word. These are the answers to your ladder!

TIP!
Underline each letter in the answers to help you write the letter clues in the next step!

HINT:
It may be helpful to first make your list of words on a piece of scratch paper.

Ladder Title

a d d
d a d
p a d
s a d
s a t
m a t
m u m
s u m

Start Here

Mystery Sentence

Copy 1

Ladder Title

9.
7.
5.
3.
1.
Start Here
8.
6.
4.
2.
Mystery Sentence

Ladder Title

8.
6.
4.
2.

Directions for students and blank templates with 7 and 9 rungs are available at scholastic.com/DWLresources.

deepen students' understanding and love of words—their structure, their meaning, and their use. Good luck and have fun with words!

—Tim and Melissa

9

Name _____

Read each clue and write the answer in the blanks.
Use the first and last words to fill in the sentence under the ladder.

HINT! Words with a ★ are more challenging!

READING & WRITING

LINES & RHYMES

11. Written or spoken language in a non-poetic form.
Add 1 letter.

_ _ _ _ _

10. A common flower.
Change 1 letter.

_ _ _ _

9. To stand a certain way for a picture.
Change 1 letter.

_ _ _ _

8. Opposite of win.
Take away 1 letter.

_ _ _ _

7. To shut.
Change 1 letter.

_ _ _ _ _

6. Past tense of choose.
Add 1 letter.

_ _ _ _ _

5. A long pipe used to water the grass.
Rearrange the letters.

_ _ _ _

4. What you wear on your foot for protection.
Add 1 letter.

_ _ _ _

3. A tool used in gardening.
Change 1 letter.

_ _ _

★ 2. Edgar Allan ____.
Take away 1 letter.

_ _ _

★ 1. Someone who writes poetry.
Take away 2 letters.

Start Here

_ _ _ _

p o e t r y

_____ has stanzas, while _____ has paragraphs.

LINES & RHYMES
Answer Key and Teaching Notes

11. Written or spoken language in a non-poetic form.

Add 1 letter.

<u>p</u> <u>r</u> <u>o</u> <u>s</u> <u>e</u>

10. A common flower.

Change 1 letter.

<u>r</u> <u>o</u> <u>s</u> <u>e</u>

9. To stand a certain way for a picture.

Change 1 letter.

<u>p</u> <u>o</u> <u>s</u> <u>e</u>

8. Opposite of *win*.

Take away 1 letter.

<u>l</u> <u>o</u> <u>s</u> <u>e</u>

7. To shut.

Change 1 letter.

Homograph: (adverb) really near someone.

<u>c</u> <u>l</u> <u>o</u> <u>s</u> <u>e</u>

6. Past tense of *choose*.

Add 1 letter.

<u>c</u> <u>h</u> <u>o</u> <u>s</u> <u>e</u>

5. A long pipe used to water the grass.

Rearrange the letters.

<u>h</u> <u>o</u> <u>s</u> <u>e</u>

4. What you wear on your foot for protection.

Add 1 letter.

<u>s</u> <u>h</u> <u>o</u> <u>e</u>

3. A tool used in gardening.

Change 1 letter.

Have students work in pairs to name other garden tools (*shovel, rake, trowel*).

<u>h</u> <u>o</u> <u>e</u>

⭐ 2. Edgar Allan ____.

Take away 1 letter.

Teach students about the famous writer best known for "The Tell-Tale Heart" and "The Raven."

<u>P</u> <u>o</u> <u>e</u>

⭐ 1. Someone who writes poetry.

Take away 2 letters.

Start Here

<u>p</u> <u>o</u> <u>e</u> <u>t</u>

p o e t r y

____<u>Poetry</u>____ has stanzas, while ____<u>prose</u>____ has paragraphs.

Name _____

Read each clue and write the answer in the blanks.
Use the first and last words to fill in the sentence under the ladder.

READING & WRITING

MAKE BELIEVE

11. A tale.
Change 2 letters.

_ _ _ _ _

10. Land along the edge of the ocean.
Add 1 letter.

_ _ _ _ _

9. What you wear on your foot for protection.
Change 1 letter.

_ _ _ _

8. I _____ an arrow from my bow.
Change 1 letter.

_ _ _ _

7. To close.
Take away the first letter, then add 2.

_ _ _ _

6. To divide with a sharp instrument.
Take away 4 letters.

_ _ _

5. Care taken to avoid danger.
Rearrange the first 2 letters, then add a vowel.

_ _ _ _ _ _ _

4. The state of doing something.
Take away 1 letter.

_ _ _ _ _ _

★ **3. A small group within a larger group.**
Take away 1 letter.

_ _ _ _ _ _ _

2. A part of a whole, used in math.
Change 1 letter.

_ _ _ _ _ _ _ _

1. A conflict, or clash of wills.
Add 1 letter.

Start Here

f i c t i o n

A _____ is often a work of _____ , meaning that it is imagined or made up.

MAKE BELIEVE
Answer Key and Teaching Notes

11. A tale.
Change 2 letters.

s t o r y

10. Land along the edge of the ocean.
Add 1 letter.

s h o r e

9. What you wear on your foot for protection.
Change 1 letter.

s h o e

8. I _____ an arrow from my bow.
Change 1 letter.
Review tenses of this verb (past: *shot*; present: *shoot*; future: *will shoot*).

s h o t

7. To close.
Take away the first letter, then add 2.
Figure of speech: *an open-and-shut case*, an obvious decision or result.

s h u t

c u t

6. To divide with a sharp instrument.
Take away 4 letters.

c a u t i o n

5. Care taken to avoid danger.
Rearrange the first 2 letters, then add a vowel.

a c t i o n

4. The state of doing something.
Take away 1 letter.

★ **3. A small group within a larger group.**
Take away 1 letter.

f a c t i o n

2. A part of a whole, used in math.
Change 1 letter.
Have students create a fraction for the number of students wearing a sweater in the class.

f r a c t i o n

1. A conflict, or clash of wills.
Add 1 letter.

Start Here

f r i c t i o n

f i c t i o n

A _____ story _____ is often a work of _____ fiction _____, meaning that it is imagined or made up.

Name _____

Read each clue and write the answer in the blanks.
Use the first and last words to fill in the sentence under the ladder.

READING & WRITING

POINTS OF VIEW!

11. First, second, ____.
Change 2 letters.

— — — — —

10. Opposite of *thin*.
Add 1 letter.

— — — — —

9. A clock goes ____ -tock.
Add 1 letter.

— — — — —

8. A game of *X*'s and *O*'s is called _____ -tac-toe.
Change 1 letter.

— — — —

7. A piece of advice.
Change 1 letter.

— — —

6. To drink a small amount at a time.
Take away 2 letters, then add 1.

— — —

5. A small piece broken off of something.
Add 1 letter.

— — — —

4. The joint at the top of your leg.
Change 1 letter.

— — —

3. Hers and ____.
Take away 1 letter.

— — —

2. ____ and that.
Take away 2 letters.

— — — —

1. The feeling of needing to drink water.
Take away the first letter, then add 2.

Start Here

— — — — —

f i r s t

A _____-person narrator tells the story as an "I," while a _____-person narrator tells the story of "he" or "she."

TIP! You may want to offer students some extra support for these more challenging words, marked with a ★.

POINTS OF VIEW!
Answer Key and Teaching Notes

11. First, second, _____.
Change 2 letters.

9. A clock goes _____ -tock.
Add 1 letter.

7. A piece of advice.
Change 1 letter.
Multiple meaning word: money given to a waiter for his or her service.

5. A small piece broken off of something.
Add 1 letter.
Figure of speech: *a chip off the old block*, a child who is very similar to his or her parent.

3. Hers and _____.
Take away 1 letter.

1. The feeling of needing to drink water.
Take away the first letter, then add 2.

Start Here

t h i r d

t h i c k

t i c k

t i c

t i p

s i p

c h i p

h i p

h i s

t h i s

t h i r s t

f i r s t

10. Opposite of *thin*.
Add 1 letter.
Figure of speech: *thick as thieves*, very close or friendly.

8. A game of *X*'s and *O*'s is called _____ -tac-toe.
Change 1 letter.

6. To drink a small amount at a time.
Take away 2 letters, then add 1.

4. The joint at the top of your leg.
Change 1 letter.
Multiple meaning word: something that is thought of as cool or trendy.

2. _____ and that.
Take away 2 letters.

A ___first___-person narrator tells the story as an "I," while a ___third___-person narrator tells the story of "he" or "she."

Name _____

Read each clue and write the answer in the blanks.
Use the first and last words to fill in the sentence under the ladder.

HINT! Words with a ★ are more challenging!

READING & WRITING

KEEP TALKING

11. Conversation between two or more people.
Add 4 letters.

_ _ _ _ _ _ _ _ _ _

10. The face of a watch or clock.
Change 1 letter.

9. An agreement.
Change 1 letter.

_ _ _ _ _

_ _ _ _

8. Common greeting in a letter.
Change 1 letter.

7. An animal with antlers.
Change 1 letter.

_ _ _ _ _

6. Opposite of *shallow*.
Change 1 letter.

_ _ _ _ _

★ **5. Slang for Vice President.**
Change 1 letter.

_ _ _ _ _

4. To change direction or turn suddenly.
Take away the prefix, then rearrange the remaining letters.

_ _ _ _ _

★ **3. To feel respect.**
Take away 1 letter.

_ _ _ _ _ _

_ _ _ _ _ _ _ _

2. To go backward.
Add 2 letters.

1. A poem or piece of poetry.
Take away 3 letters.

_ _ _ _ _

Start Here

c o n v e r s e

When characters in a story _____ , the writer formats their words as _____ , with quotation marks around the words spoken.

KEEP TALKING
Answer Key and Teaching Notes

d i a l o g u e

11. Conversation between two or more people.
Add 4 letters.

d i a l

10. The face of a watch or clock.
Change 1 letter.

d e a l

9. An agreement.
Change 1 letter.

d e a r

8. Common greeting in a letter.
Change 1 letter.
Homophone: *deer*.

d e e r

7. An animal with antlers.
Change 1 letter.
Figure of speech: *deer in headlights*, when someone looks surprised or taken aback.

d e e p

6. Opposite of *shallow*.
Change 1 letter.
Figure of speech: *deep pockets*, has a lot of money.

V e e p

⭐ 5. Slang for Vice President.
Change 1 letter.

v e e r

4. To change direction or turn suddenly.
Take away the prefix, then rearrange the remaining letters.

r e v e r e

⭐ 3. To feel respect.
Take away 1 letter.

r e v e r s e

2. To go backward.
Add 2 letters.

v e r s e

1. A poem or piece of poetry.
Take away 3 letters.

Start Here

c o n v e r s e

When characters in a story __converse__, the writer formats their words as __dialogue__, with quotation marks around the words spoken.

Name _____

Read each clue and write the answer in the blanks.
Use the first and last words to fill in the sentence under the ladder.

READING & WRITING

BAD GUYS

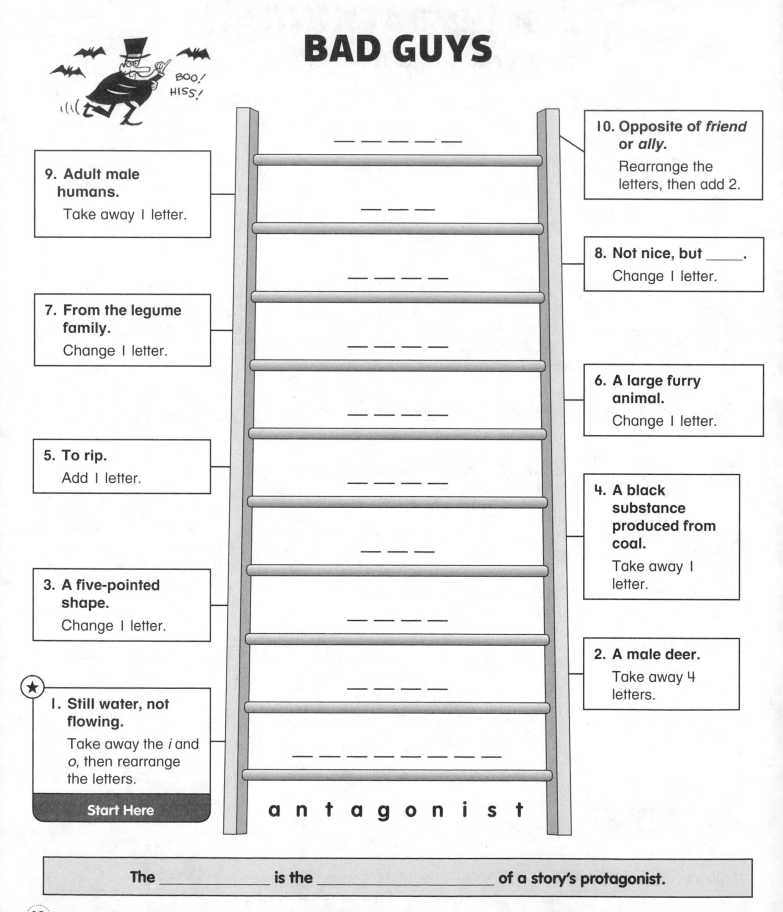

BOO! HISS!

9. Adult male humans.
Take away 1 letter.

7. From the legume family.
Change 1 letter.

5. To rip.
Add 1 letter.

3. A five-pointed shape.
Change 1 letter.

★ 1. Still water, not flowing.
Take away the *i* and *o*, then rearrange the letters.

Start Here

_ _ _ _ _ _

_ _ _

_ _ _ _

_ _ _ _

_ _ _ _

_ _ _ _

_ _ _

_ _ _ _

_ _ _ _

_ _ _ _ _ _ _ _ _

a n t a g o n i s t

10. Opposite of *friend* or *ally*.
Rearrange the letters, then add 2.

8. Not nice, but ____.
Change 1 letter.

6. A large furry animal.
Change 1 letter.

4. A black substance produced from coal.
Take away 1 letter.

2. A male deer.
Take away 4 letters.

The _____ is the _____ of a story's protagonist.

TIP! You may want to offer students some extra support for these more challenging words, marked with a ⊛.

BAD GUYS
Answer Key and Teaching Notes

BOO! HISS!

9. Adult male humans.
Take away 1 letter.

7. From the legume family.
Change 1 letter.
Have students work in pairs to name types of beans (*navy, pinto, black, fava*).

5. To rip.
Add 1 letter.
Homograph: (noun) what the eye produces when crying.

3. A five-pointed shape.
Change 1 letter.

⊛ 1. Still water, not flowing.
Take away the *i* and *o*, then rearrange the letters.

Start Here

e n e m y

m e n

m e a n

b e a n

b e a r

t e a r

t a r

s t a r

s t a g

s t a g n a n t

a n t a g o n i s t

10. Opposite of *friend* or *ally*.
Rearrange the letters, then add 2.

8. Not nice, but _____.
Change 1 letter.

6. A large furry animal.
Change 1 letter.
Multiple meaning word: to hold up and support (*bear the weight*).

4. A black substance produced from coal.
Take away 1 letter.

2. A male deer.
Take away 4 letters.

The ___antagonist___ is the ___enemy___ of a story's protagonist.

Read each clue and write the answer in the blanks.
Use the first and last words to fill in the sentence under the ladder.

READING & WRITING

FINDING THE WAY

11. The answer to a problem.
Add 2 letters (*s, u*), then rearrange.

10. Cream to help relieve dry skin.
Change 1 letter.

9. An idea.
Change 1 letter.

8. A territory or country.
Change 2 letters.

★ **7. Belonging by birth.**
Add 2 letters.

★ **6. The central part of a church building.**
Change 1 letter.

5. To talk wildly and excitedly about.
Take away 1 letter.

4. To want badly.
Take away 1 letter, then add 2.

3. To overstuff something.
Change 1 letter.

★ **2. Another name for a baby stroller.**
Change 1 letter.

1. An end-of-year dance for high school students.
Take away 3 letters.

Start Here

p r o b l e m

A story starts with a _____ and ends with a _____.

FINDING THE WAY
Answer Key and Teaching Notes

11. The answer to a problem.
Add 2 letters (*s, u*), then rearrange.

s o l u t i o n

10. Cream to help relieve dry skin.
Change 1 letter.
Have students guess the year sunscreen lotion was invented (1936).

l o t i o n

9. An idea.
Change 1 letter.

n o t i o n

★ **7. Belonging by birth.**
Add 2 letters.
Discuss how Native Americans were the first to inhabit the United States.

n a t i o n

8. A territory or country.
Change 2 letters.

n a t i v e

5. To talk wildly and excitedly about.
Take away 1 letter.

n a v e

★ **6. The central part of a church building.**
Change 1 letter.
Show students a digital image of a nave.

r a v e

3. To overstuff something.
Change 1 letter.

c r a v e

4. To want badly.
Take away 1 letter, then add 2.

c r a m

1. An end-of-year dance for high school students.
Take away 3 letters.

Start Here

p r a m

★ **2. Another name for a baby stroller.**
Change 1 letter.

p r o m

p r o b l e m

A story starts with a ____problem____ and ends with a ____solution____.

Name _____

Read each clue and write the answer in the blanks.
Use the first and last words to fill in the sentence under the ladder.

HINT! Words with a ⭐ are more challenging!

READING & WRITING

WORDS TO THE WISE

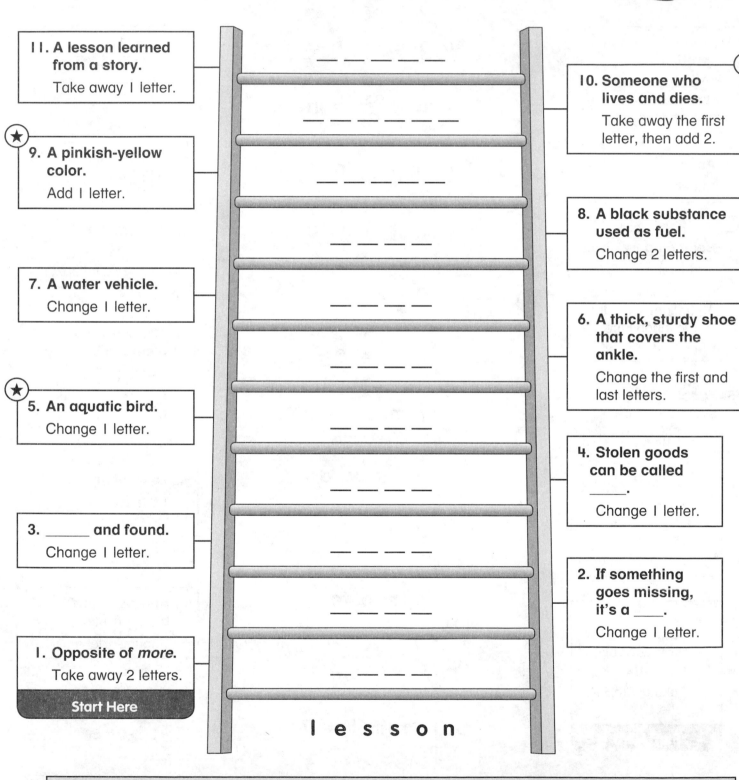

11. A lesson learned from a story.
Take away 1 letter.

_ _ _ _ _ _

⭐ **10. Someone who lives and dies.**
Take away the first letter, then add 2.

⭐ **9. A pinkish-yellow color.**
Add 1 letter.

_ _ _ _ _ _ _

8. A black substance used as fuel.
Change 2 letters.

_ _ _ _ _ _

7. A water vehicle.
Change 1 letter.

_ _ _ _

6. A thick, sturdy shoe that covers the ankle.
Change the first and last letters.

_ _ _ _

⭐ **5. An aquatic bird.**
Change 1 letter.

_ _ _ _

4. Stolen goods can be called _____.
Change 1 letter.

_ _ _ _

3. _____ and found.
Change 1 letter.

_ _ _ _

2. If something goes missing, it's a ____.
Change 1 letter.

_ _ _ _

1. Opposite of *more*.
Take away 2 letters.

Start Here

_ _ _ _

l e s s o n

The _____ of a story is the _____ learned from the characters' actions.

22

TIP! You may want to offer students some extra support for these more challenging words, marked with a ⭐.

WORDS TO THE WISE
Answer Key and Teaching Notes

11. A lesson learned from a story.
Take away 1 letter.

9. A pinkish-yellow color. ⭐
Add 1 letter.
Multiple meaning word: skeletons that form reefs.

7. A water vehicle.
Change 1 letter.

5. An aquatic bird. ⭐
Change 1 letter.

3. _____ and found.
Change 1 letter.

1. Opposite of *more*.
Take away 2 letters.

Start Here

10. Someone who lives and dies. ⭐
Take away the first letter, then add 2.

8. A black substance used as fuel.
Change 2 letters.

6. A thick, sturdy shoe that covers the ankle.
Change the first and last letters.

4. Stolen goods can be called _____.
Change 1 letter.
Have students list synonyms for *money* (*cash, wealth, capital, bills*).

2. If something goes missing, it's a ____.
Change 1 letter.
Figure of speech: *at a loss for words*, when you don't know what to say or do in a situation.

m o r a l

m o r t a l

c o r a l

c o a l

b o a t

b o o t

l o o n

l o o t

l o s t

l o s s

l e s s

l e s s o n

The ___moral___ of a story is the ___lesson___ learned from the characters' actions.

Name _____

Read each clue and write the answer in the blanks.
Use the first and last words to fill in the sentence under the ladder.

STORYTELLERS

10. Someone who creates stories.
Add 2 letters.

★ **9. A ceremonial act, sometimes religious.**
Change 1 letter.

★ **8. To irritate.**
Change the first vowel, then rearrange the letters.

7. To attract.
Change 1 letter.

★ **6. A one- or two-person sled.**
Add 1 letter.

5. To carry along with a lot of effort.
Change 1 letter.

4. To pull on something.
Take away 3 letters.

3. Past tense of *teach*.
Add 2 letters.

2. Stretched or pulled tight.
Change 1 letter, then rearrange the letters.

1. Short for *automobile*.
Take away 2 letters.

Start Here

a u t h o r

The _____ of a book is formally known as the _____.

24

TIP! You may want to offer students some extra support for these more challenging words, marked with a ★.

STORYTELLERS
Answer Key and Teaching Notes

w r i t e r

r i t e

r i l e

l u r e

l u g e

l u g

t u g

t a u g h t

t a u t

a u t o

a u t h o r

★ 9. A ceremonial act, sometimes religious.

Change 1 letter.

7. To attract.

Change 1 letter.

5. To carry along with a lot of effort.

Change 1 letter.

3. Past tense of *teach*.

Add 2 letters.

Discuss tenses of this word (past: *taught*; present: *teach*; future: *will teach*).

1. Short for *automobile*.

Take away 2 letters.

Start Here

10. Someone who creates stories.

Add 2 letters.

Figure of speech: *writer's block*, inability to write for lack of ideas.

★ 8. To irritate.

Change the first vowel, then rearrange the letters.

★ 6. A one- or two-person sled.

Add 1 letter.

Show students a digital image of a luge.

4. To pull on something.

Take away 3 letters.

2. Stretched or pulled tight.

Change 1 letter, then rearrange the letters.

The ___writer___ of a book is formally known as the ___author___.

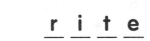

Name _____

Read each clue and write the answer in the blanks.
Use the first and last words to fill in the sentence under the ladder.

HINT! Words with a ⭐ are more challenging!

READING & WRITING

BIRD'S EYE VIEW

11. To use your finger to bring attention to something.
Add 1 letter.

— — — — —

10. Two cups equal one ____.
Change 1 letter.

9. A clue.
Change 1 letter.

— — — —

8. The handle of a sword or weapon. ⭐
Change 1 letter.

7. A natural rise in the earth's surface.
Change 1 letter.

— — — —

— — — —

6. A green plant used to flavor food.
Change 2 letters.

5. A business transaction.
Change 2 letters.

— — — —

— — — —

4. An animal with antlers.
Change 1 letter.

3. To change direction.
Rearrange the letters, then add 1.

— — — —

2. To press the gas pedal in a vehicle.
Take away 3 letters.

— — —

1. To look over something again.
Add 2 letters.

Start Here

— — — — — —

v i e w

We read a story through the narrator's _____ of _____, which shows us her or his thoughts and opinions.

TIP! You may want to offer students some extra support for these more challenging words, marked with a ⭐.

BIRD'S EYE VIEW
Answer Key and Teaching Notes

11. To use your finger to bring attention to something.
Add 1 letter.

p o i n t

10. Two cups equal one _____.
Change 1 letter.

p i n t

9. A clue.
Change 1 letter.

h i n t

⭐
8. The handle of a sword or weapon.
Change 1 letter.
Show students a digital image of a hilt.

h i l t

7. A natural rise in the earth's surface.
Change 1 letter.

h i l l

6. A green plant used to flavor food.
Change 2 letters.

d i l l

5. A business transaction.
Change 2 letters.

d e a l

4. An animal with antlers.
Change 1 letter.

d e e r

3. To change direction.
Rearrange the letters, then add 1.

v e e r

2. To press the gas pedal in a vehicle.
Take away 3 letters.

r e v

1. To look over something again.
Add 2 letters.
Have students list other words with the prefix re- (redo, rework, react).

r e v i e w

Start Here

v i e w

We read a story through the narrator's _____point_____ of _____view_____, which shows us her or his thoughts and opinions.

Read each clue and write the answer in the blanks.
Use the first and last words to fill in the sentence under the ladder.

READING & WRITING

WHAT'S THE BIG IDEA?

friendship *COURAGE* *SURVIVAL*

10. Subject.
Take away 1 letter.

★ **9. The _____ of Capricorn.**
Take away 3 letters, then add 2.

8. Vehicles on a road.
Take away 3 letters (*e, r, i*), then add 2.

7. Another word for *great*.
Take away the last 2 letters, then add 3.

6. A breed of dog. ★
Add 3 letters.

★ **5. A row or level.**
Change 1 letter.

4. When a game ends and the score is even on both sides.
Add 1 letter.

3. Carlos learned how to _____ his shoes in kindergarten.
Change 1 letter.

2. _____ Three Little Pigs.
Take away 1 letter.

1. A pronoun: I asked _____ if I could play.
Take away 1 letter.

Start Here

t h e m e

The _____ is the central message or _____ of a story.

TIP! You may want to offer students some extra support for these more challenging words, marked with a ★.

WHAT'S THE BIG IDEA?

Friendship
COURAGE
SURVIVAL

Answer Key and Teaching Notes

t o p i c

T r o p i c

t r a f f i c

t e r r i f i c

t e r r i e r

t i e r

t i e d

t i e

T h e

t h e m

t h e m e

★ **9. The _____ of Capricorn.**
Take away 3 letters, then add 2.
Show students a digital image of the Tropic of Capricorn on a map.

7. Another word for *great*.
Take away the last 2 letters, then add 3.
Have students list synonyms for *terrific* (*awesome, excellent, fantastic*).

★ **5. A row or level.**
Change 1 letter.

3. Carlos learned how to ____ his shoes in kindergarten.
Change 1 letter.

1. A pronoun: I asked ____ if I could play.
Take away 1 letter.

Start Here

10. Subject.
Take away 1 letter.

8. Vehicles on a road.
Take away 3 letters (*e, r, i*), then add 2.

★ **6. A breed of dog.**
Add 3 letters.

4. When a game ends and the score is even on both sides.
Add 1 letter.
Review tenses of this word (past: *tied*; present: *tie*; future: *will tie*).

2. ____ Three Little Pigs.
Take away 1 letter.

The ___theme___ is the central message or ___topic___ of a story.

Name _____

Read each clue and write the answer in the blanks.
Use the first and last words to fill in the sentence under the ladder.

HINT! Words with a ★ are more challenging!

READING & WRITING

THAT'S MY POINT

11. A disagreement.
Add 3 letters.

— — — — — — — —

10. To dispute.
Add 1 letter, then rearrange the letters.

— — — — — —

9. To push someone to do something.
Take away 1 letter.

— — — —

8. A forward rush of something. ★
Change 1 letter.

— — — — —

★ **7. To get rid of or throw away.**
Add 1 letter.

— — — — — —

6. Free from mixture.
Change 1 letter.

— — — — —

5. To attract.
Change 2 letters.

— — — —

4. A straight or curved mark.
Change the last letter, then add 1.

— — — —

3. A place that provides lodging.
Change 1 letter.

— — —

★ **2. An electrically charged atom.**
Take away 2 letters.

— — —

1. Vegetable with a strong flavor used a lot in cooking.
Take away 2 letters.

Start Here

— — — — —

o p i n i o n

When presenting your _____, you can provide both facts and _____s.

THAT'S MY POINT
Answer Key and Teaching Notes

11. A disagreement.
Add 3 letters.

a r g u m e n t

10. To dispute.
Add 1 letter, then rearrange the letters.
Have students list synonyms for *argue* (*disagree, dispute, squabble, quarrel*).

9. To push someone to do something.
Take away 1 letter.

a r g u e

u r g e

★ **7. To get rid of or throw away.**
Add 1 letter.
Have students list synonyms for *purge* (*cleanse, remove*).

s u r g e

★ **8. A forward rush of something.**
Change 1 letter.

p u r g e

5. To attract.
Change 2 letters.

p u r e

6. Free from mixture.
Change 1 letter.

l u r e

3. A place that provides lodging.
Change 1 letter.
Homophone: *in*, the opposite of *out*.

l i n e

4. A straight or curved mark.
Change the last letter, then add 1.

i n n

1. Vegetable with a strong flavor used a lot in cooking.
Take away 2 letters.

i o n

★ **2. An electrically charged atom.**
Take away 2 letters.

o n i o n

Start Here

o p i n i o n

When presenting your ___argument___, you can provide both facts and ___opinion___s.

Name _____

Read each clue and write the answer in the blanks.
Use the first and last words to fill in the sentence under the ladder.

READING & WRITING

APPLES & ORANGES

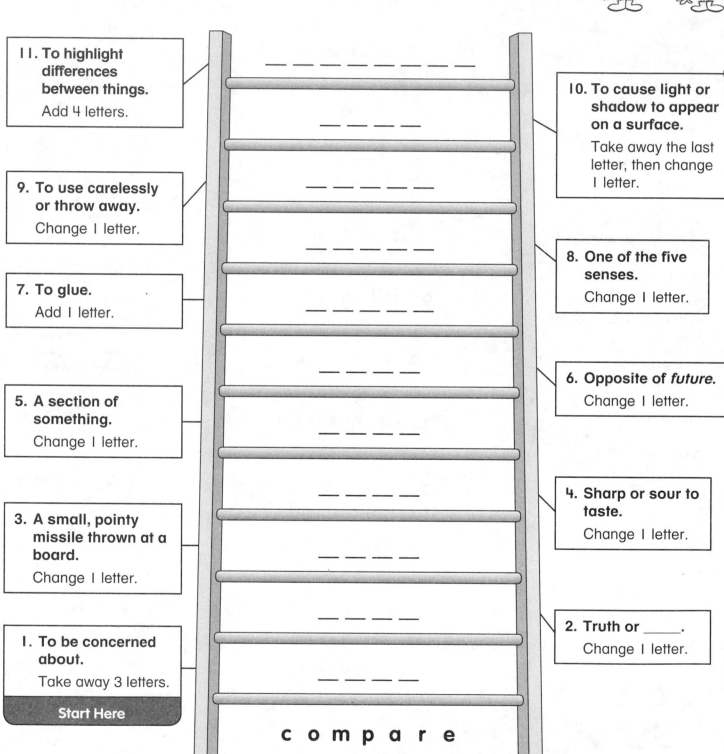

11. To highlight differences between things.
Add 4 letters.

9. To use carelessly or throw away.
Change 1 letter.

7. To glue.
Add 1 letter.

5. A section of something.
Change 1 letter.

3. A small, pointy missile thrown at a board.
Change 1 letter.

1. To be concerned about.
Take away 3 letters.

Start Here

★ 10. To cause light or shadow to appear on a surface.
Take away the last letter, then change 1 letter.

8. One of the five senses.
Change 1 letter.

6. Opposite of *future*.
Change 1 letter.

4. Sharp or sour to taste.
Change 1 letter.

2. Truth or _____.
Change 1 letter.

c o m p a r e

To show how things are similar, _____ them; to show how things are different, _____ them.

TIP! You may want to offer students some extra support for these more challenging words, marked with a ★.

READING & WRITING

APPLES & ORANGES
Answer Key and Teaching Notes

contrast

11. To highlight differences between things.
Add 4 letters.

c a s t

10. To cause light or shadow to appear on a surface. ★
Take away the last letter, then change 1 letter.

w a s t e

9. To use carelessly or throw away.
Change 1 letter.

t a s t e

8. One of the five senses.
Change 1 letter.

p a s t e

7. To glue.
Add 1 letter.

p a s t

6. Opposite of *future*.
Change 1 letter.
Have students list synonyms for *past* (*completed, prior, former*).

p a r t

5. A section of something.
Change 1 letter.

t a r t

4. Sharp or sour to taste.
Change 1 letter.

d a r t

3. A small, pointy missile thrown at a board.
Change 1 letter.

d a r e

2. Truth or _____.
Change 1 letter.
Figure of speech: *you wouldn't dare*, disbelief in what someone is saying he is going to do.

c a r e

1. To be concerned about.
Take away 3 letters.

Start Here

c o m p a r e

To show how things are similar, ___compare___ them; to show how things are different, ___contrast___ them.

33

Read each clue and write the answer in the blanks.
Use the first and last words to fill in the sentence under the ladder.

READING & WRITING

GUESS WHAT?

11. To guess what is going to happen.

Add 2 letters, then rearrange.

— — — — — — —

10. The feeling of being proud.

Add 1 letter.

— — — — —

9. Present tense of *rode*.

Change 1 letter.

— — — —

8. The traveling band ____ in the back of a big bus.

Change 2 letters.

— — — —

7. I wanted to get ____ of my shoes because they were too small. To throw away.

Change 1 letter, then rearrange.

— — —

6. A slight downward motion.

Change 1 letter.

— — —

★ **5. A loud, confused noise.**

Change 1 letter.

— — —

4. A shelter for a wild animal.

Take away 2 letters.

— — —

3. Packed closely together.

Change 2 letters.

— — — — —

2. A barrier enclosing a yard.

Take away 7 letters.

— — — — —

★ **1. In football, when players run ahead to block other players.**

Add 3 letters.

Start Here

— — — — — — — — — — — —

i n f e r e n c e

When you make an _____ , you _____ what will happen in a text.

GUESS WHAT?
Answer Key and Teaching Notes

TIP! You may want to offer students some extra support for these more challenging words, marked with a ★.

11. To guess what is going to happen.
Add 2 letters, then rearrange.

9. Present tense of *rode*.
Change 1 letter.

7. I wanted to get ____ of my shoes because they were too small. To throw away.
Change 1 letter, then rearrange.

★ **5. A loud, confused noise.**
Change 1 letter.

3. Packed closely together.
Change 2 letters.
Have students list synonyms for *dense* (*thick, crowded, compressed*).

★ **1. In football, when players run ahead to block other players.**
Add 3 letters.

Start Here

p r e d i c t

p r i d e

r i d e

r o d e

r i d

d i p

d i n

d e n

d e n s e

f e n c e

i n t e r f e r e n c e

i n f e r e n c e

10. The feeling of being proud.
Add 1 letter.

8. The traveling band ____ in the back of a big bus.
Change 2 letters.
Review verb tenses (past: *rode*, present: *ride*, future: *will ride*).

6. A slight downward motion.
Change 1 letter.
Multiple meaning word: a sauce to dip vegetables into.

4. A shelter for a wild animal.
Take away 2 letters.

2. A barrier enclosing a yard.
Take away 7 letters.

When you make an ___inference___, you ___predict___ what will happen in a text.

Name _____

Read each clue and write the answer in the blanks.
Use the first and last words to fill in the sentence under the ladder.

READING & WRITING

SHARING NOTES

11. A secondary meaning of a word, often positive or negative.
Add 3 letters.

9. A country or group of people.
Change 1 letter.

7. A fun trip away from home.
Take away the *e*, then add 3 letters.

5. A hollow in the earth.
Change 2 letters.

3. A sound, often musical.
Rearrange the letters.

★
1. To be a sign of.
Take away 5 letters, then add 1.
Start Here

10. A system of symbols other than ordinary writing. ★
Add 2 letters.

8. An allotted amount of something. ★
Take away the first 3 letters, then add 1.

6. To leave an area.
Add 2 letters, then rearrange.

4. We bought an ice cream _____.
Change 1 letter.

2. A short and informal message.
Take away 2 letters.

d e n o t a t i o n

Every word has a specific _____, or meaning, but the _____ is often the feeling or idea that a word invokes or suggests.

36

SHARING NOTES
Answer Key and Teaching Notes

11. A secondary meaning of a word, often positive or negative.
Add 3 letters.

c o n n o t a t i o n

(★) 10. A system of symbols other than ordinary writing.
Add 2 letters.

n o t a t i o n

9. A country or group of people.
Change 1 letter.

n a t i o n

(★) 8. An allotted amount of something.
Take away the first 3 letters, then add 1.

r a t i o n

7. A fun trip away from home.
Take away the *e*, then add 3 letters.

v a c a t i o n

6. To leave an area.
Add 2 letters, then rearrange.
Have students list synonyms for *vacate* (*abandon, evacuate*).

v a c a t e

5. A hollow in the earth.
Change 2 letters.

c a v e

4. We bought an ice cream _____.
Change 1 letter.
Have students name common items shaped like cones (*funnel, party hat, ice cream cone, Christmas tree*).

c o n e

3. A sound, often musical.
Rearrange the letters.
Figure of speech: *to set the tone*, to establish a certain mood.

t o n e

(★) 1. To be a sign of.
Take away 5 letters, then add 1.

Start Here

n o t e

2. A short and informal message.
Take away 2 letters.

d e n o t e

d e n o t a t i o n

Every word has a specific __denotation__, or meaning, but the __connotation__ is often the feeling or idea that a word invokes or suggests.

Name _____

Read each clue and write the answer in the blanks.
Use the first and last words to fill in the sentence under the ladder.

REAL OR NOT?

11. A made-up story.
Change 1 letter.

_ _ _ _ _ _ _

10. A group within a larger group. ★
Add 1 letter.

_ _ _ _ _ _ _

9. The process of doing something.
Add 3 letters.

_ _ _ _ _ _

8. Part of a play.
Take away 1 letter.

_ _ _

7. A sense of what is appropriate to say. ★
Change 1 letter.

_ _ _ _

6. An agreement between two or more people or parties.
Change 1 letter.

_ _ _ _

5. The rate of movement.
Take away the first 2 letters, then add 1.

_ _ _ _

4. Favor or goodwill.
Change 1 letter.

_ _ _ _ _

3. To follow the track of something with a finger or pen.
Add 1 letter.

_ _ _ _ _

2. A contest of speed.
Change 1 letter.

_ _ _ _

1. The front part of your head.
Change 1 letter.

Start Here

_ _ _ _

f a c t

Something invented is a _____, while something true is a _____.

TIP! You may want to offer students some extra support for these more challenging words, marked with a ★.

REAL OR NOT?
Answer Key and Teaching Notes

11. A made-up story.
Change 1 letter.

9. The process of doing something.
Add 3 letters.

★ **7. A sense of what is appropriate to say.**
Change 1 letter.

5. The rate of movement.
Take away the first 2 letters, then add 1.
Figure of speech: *a change of pace*, a change in routine.

3. To follow the track of something with a finger or pen.
Add 1 letter.

1. The front part of your head.
Change 1 letter.
Figure of speech: *face the music*, to take responsibility for one's actions.

Start Here

f i c t i o n

f a c t i o n

a c t i o n

a c t

t a c t

p a c t

p a c e

g r a c e

t r a c e

r a c e

f a c e

f a c t

★ **10. A group within a larger group.**
Add 1 letter.
Have students determine the number of syllables (vowel sounds) in the word.

8. Part of a play.
Take away 1 letter.

6. An agreement between two or more people or parties.
Change 1 letter.

4. Favor or goodwill.
Change 1 letter.

2. A contest of speed.
Change 1 letter.

Something invented is a ___fiction___, while something true is a ___fact___.

Name _____

Read each clue and write the answer in the blanks.
Use the first and last words to fill in the sentence under the ladder.

HINT! Words with a ⭐ are more challenging!

READING & WRITING

APPLES TO APPLES

11. "He is as hungry as a lion" is a _____.

Add 1 letter.

_ _ _ _ _

10. Opposite of _frown_.

Add 1 letter.

_ _ _ _ _ _

9. My grandma lives 30 ____s away.

Change 1 letter.

_ _ _ _

8. Opposite of _female_.

Change 1 letter.

_ _ _ _

7. "Cinderella" is a fairy _____.

Take away 1 letter.

_ _ _ _ _

6. Old bread or crackers taste ____.

Change 1 letter.

_ _ _ _ _ _

5. A pointed stick or post driven into the ground.

Add 1 letter.

_ _ _ _

4. "For goodness' ____!"

Take away 1 letter.

3. To move with short, quick movements.

Change 2 letters.

_ _ _ _

2. A small, thin piece of something.

Add 1 letter.

_ _ _ _ _

1. A body of water surrounded by land.

Change 1 letter.

Start Here

l i k e

A _____ is a comparison that has the word _____ or _as_ in it.

TIP! You may want to offer students some extra support for these more challenging words, marked with a ⭐.

READING & WRITING

APPLES TO APPLES
Answer Key and Teaching Notes

11. "He is as hungry as a lion" is a _____.
Add 1 letter.

s i m i l e

10. Opposite of *frown*.
Add 1 letter.

s m i l e

9. My grandma lives 30 ____s away.
Change 1 letter.

m i l e

8. Opposite of *female*.
Change 1 letter.

m a l e

7. "Cinderella" is a fairy ____.
Take away 1 letter.
Homophone: *tail*, a back-end part of some animals.

t a l e

5. A pointed stick or post driven into the ground.
Add 1 letter.
Homophone: *steak*, a common edible red meat.

s t a l e

6. Old bread or crackers taste ____.
Change 1 letter.

s t a k e

4. "For goodness' __!"
Take away 1 letter.

s a k e

3. To move with short, quick movements.
Change 2 letters.

s h a k e

2. A small, thin piece of something.
Add 1 letter.

f l a k e

1. A body of water surrounded by land.
Change 1 letter.

Start Here

l a k e

l i k e

A ___simile___ is a comparison that has the word ___like___ or *as* in it.

Name _____

Read each clue and write the answer in the blanks.
Use the first and last words to fill in the sentence under the ladder.

HINT! Words with a ⭐ are more challenging!

READING & WRITING

DO YOU MEAN TO SAY...?

11. To note similarities.
Add 3 letters.

__ __ __ __ __ __ __

10. To cut off the outer layer of a fruit or vegetable.
Rearrange the letters.

__ __ __ __

9. A fruit.
Change 1 letter.

__ __ __ __

8. The first word when you write a letter to someone.
Rearrange the letters.

__ __ __ __

7. To look at and understand words.
Take away 1 letter.

__ __ __ __

6. To fear something that is going to happen. ⭐
Change 1 letter.

5. To walk in a specific way.
Change 1 letter, then add 1.

__ __ __ __ __

4. Past tense of *tread* (walk). ⭐
Change 1 letter.

__ __ __ __ __ __

3. For a horse, between a walk and a run.
Take away 1 letter, then add 1.

__ __ __ __

2. A mechanical or habitual procedure. ⭐
Take away the first 2 letters, then rearrange the remaining letters.

__ __ __ __

1. A body of matter from outer space.
Take away 3 letters (*a, p, h*), then add 1.

Start Here

__ __ __ __ __ __

m e t a p h o r

A _____ challenges the reader to _____ two unrelated things.

TIP! You may want to offer students some extra support for these more challenging words, marked with a ★.

DO YOU MEAN TO SAY...?

Answer Key and Teaching Notes

c o m p a r e

11. To note similarities.
Add 3 letters.

p a r e

10. To cut off the outer layer of a fruit or vegetable.
Rearrange the letters.
Homophones: *pear, pair.*

p e a r

9. A fruit.
Change 1 letter.

d e a r

8. The first word when you write a letter to someone.
Rearrange the letters.

r e a d

7. To look at and understand words.
Take away 1 letter.

d r e a d

6. To fear something that is going to happen. ★
Change 1 letter.

t r e a d

5. To walk in a specific way.
Change 1 letter, then add 1.
Review the past tense of *tread* (*trod*).

t r o d

4. Past tense of *tread* (walk). ★
Change 1 letter.

t r o t

3. For a horse, between a walk and a run.
Take away 1 letter, then add 1.

r o t e

2. A mechanical or habitual procedure. ★
Take away the first 2 letters, then rearrange the remaining letters.

m e t e o r

1. A body of matter from outer space.
Take away 3 letters (*a, p, h*), then add 1.

Start Here

m e t a p h o r

A metaphor challenges the reader to compare two unrelated things.

Name _____

Read each clue and write the answer in the blanks.
Use the first and last words to fill in the sentence under the ladder.

READING & WRITING

HELLO! GOODBYE!

10. The ending of something.
Take away the first 2 letters, then add 3.

⭐ 9. The state of being isolated.
Take away the last 2 letters, then add 4.

⭐ 8. To shut away or isolate.
Add 2 letters, then rearrange.

7. A type of leather with a soft surface.
Add 2 letters.

6. Short for *Susan*.
Change 1 letter.

5. What is owed at the present time.
Take away 1 letter.

4. A song sung by two people.
Change 1 letter.

3. A formal fight between two people.
Take away the second *d*, then add 1 letter.

2. Another name for a man or a guy.
Change 2 letters.

⭐ 1. A tube or passageway.
Take away the prefix and the suffix.

Start Here

i n t r o d u c t i o n

In formal writing, the beginning is called the _____, and the ending is called the _____.

TIP! You may want to offer students some extra support for these more challenging words, marked with a ★.

HELLO! GOODBYE!
Answer Key and Teaching Notes

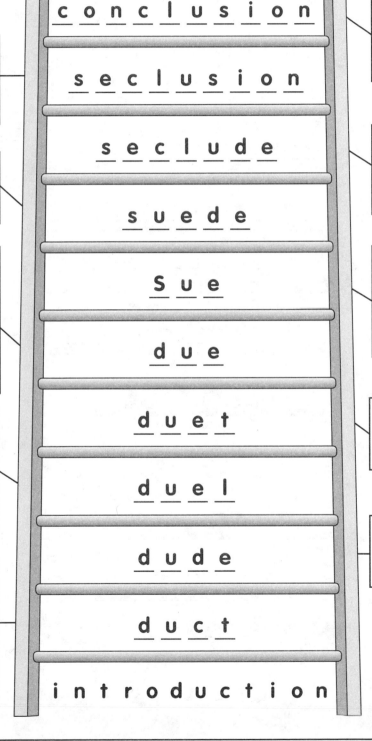

9. The state of being isolated.
Take away the last 2 letters, then add 4.

7. A type of leather with a soft surface.
Add 2 letters.

5. What is owed at the present time.
Take away 1 letter.
Figure of speech: *to give someone her due*, give someone credit for her work.

3. A formal fight between two people.
Take away the second *d*, then add 1 letter.

★ **1. A tube or passageway.**
Take away the prefix and the suffix.

Start Here

Ladder (top to bottom):
c o n c l u s i o n
s e c l u s i o n
s e c l u d e
s u e d e
S u e
d u e
d u e t
d u e l
d u d e
d u c t
i n t r o d u c t i o n

10. The ending of something.
Take away the first 2 letters, then add 3.

★ **8. To shut away or isolate.**
Add 2 letters, then rearrange.

6. Short for *Susan*.
Change 1 letter.
Multiple meaning word: to bring court action against.

4. A song sung by two people.
Change 1 letter.

2. Another name for a man or a guy.
Change 2 letters.

In formal writing, the beginning is called the ___introduction___, and the ending is called the ___conclusion___.

Name _____

Read each clue and write the answer in the blanks.
Use the first and last words to fill in the sentence under the ladder.

READING & WRITING

PARTS OF A WHOLE

11. Groups of words that each form a thought.
Add 5 letters to the end.

⭐ **9. Short for *gentleman*.**
Change 1 letter.

7. A payment made to use another person's property, such as a home.
Change 1 letter.

5. To make a deep, guttural sound.
Change 2 letters.

⭐ **3. To reduce to small shreds, like cheese.**
Change 1 letter.

1. A diagram that shows data or connections.
Take away 4 letters.

Start Here

10. Past tense of *send*.
Change 1 letter.

8. Dollars and ____s.
Change 1 letter.

6. The smallest in a litter of dogs.
Take away 1 letter.

4. Very good.
Rearrange the last 3 letters.

2. A fruit that grows in clusters.
Change 1 letter.

p a r a g r a p h

A _____ is made up of related _____.

PARTS OF A WHOLE
Answer Key and Teaching Notes

11. Groups of words that each form a thought.
Add 5 letters to the end.

s e n t e n c e s

10. Past tense of *send*.
Change 1 letter.

s e n t

★ **9. Short for *gentleman*.**
Change 1 letter.

g e n t

8. Dollars and ____s.
Change 1 letter.
Ask students to name who is on the penny (*A. Lincoln*), nickel (*T. Jefferson*), dime (*F.D. Roosevelt*), and quarter (*G. Washington*).

c e n t

7. A payment made to use another person's property, such as a home.
Change 1 letter.

r e n t

r u n t

6. The smallest in a litter of dogs.
Take away 1 letter.

5. To make a deep, guttural sound.
Change 2 letters.
Figure of speech: *grunt work*, simple, repetitive work.

g r u n t

g r e a t

4. Very good.
Rearrange the last 3 letters.

★ **3. To reduce to small shreds, like cheese.**
Change 1 letter.

g r a t e

g r a p e

2. A fruit that grows in clusters.
Change 1 letter.

1. A diagram that shows data or connections.
Take away 4 letters.

g r a p h

Start Here

p a r a g r a p h

A ___paragraph___ is made up of related ___sentences___.

Name _____

Read each clue and write the answer in the blanks.
Use the first and last words to fill in the sentence under the ladder.

HINT! Words with a ★ are more challenging!

READING & WRITING

CHANGE IT UP

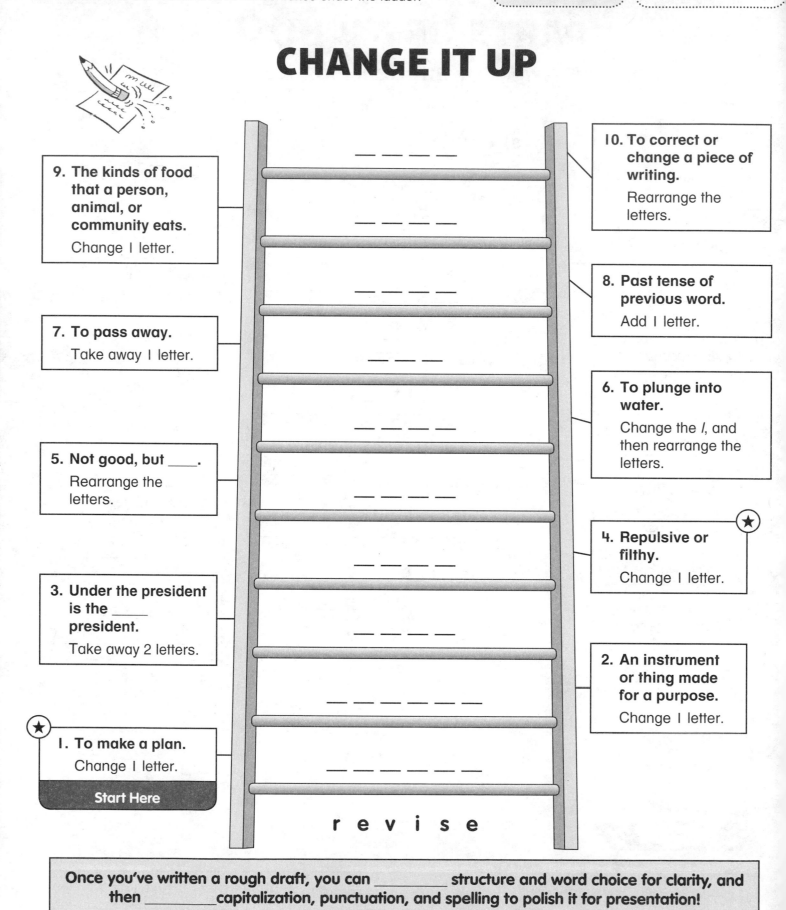

9. The kinds of food that a person, animal, or community eats.

Change I letter.

7. To pass away.

Take away I letter.

5. Not good, but ____.

Rearrange the letters.

3. Under the president is the _____ president.

Take away 2 letters.

★

1. To make a plan.

Change I letter.

Start Here

10. To correct or change a piece of writing.

Rearrange the letters.

8. Past tense of previous word.

Add I letter.

6. To plunge into water.

Change the *l*, and then rearrange the letters.

★ **4.** Repulsive or filthy.

Change I letter.

2. An instrument or thing made for a purpose.

Change I letter.

r e v i s e

Once you've written a rough draft, you can _____ structure and word choice for clarity, and then _____ capitalization, punctuation, and spelling to polish it for presentation!

CHANGE IT UP
Answer Key and Teaching Notes

e d i t

d i e t

d i e d

d i e

d i v e

e v i l

v i l e

v i c e

d e v i c e

d e v i s e

r e v i s e

Start Here

9. **The kinds of food that a person, animal, or community eats.**
Change 1 letter.

7. **To pass away.**
Take away 1 letter.

5. **Not good, but _____.**
Rearrange the letters.

3. **Under the president is the _____ president.**
Take away 2 letters.
Multiple meaning word: a bad habit.

★ 1. **To make a plan.**
Change 1 letter.

10. **To correct or change a piece of writing.**
Rearrange the letters.

8. **Past tense of previous word.**
Add 1 letter.

6. **To plunge into water.**
Change the *l*, and then rearrange the letters.
Figure of speech: *dive in*, to throw yourself into doing a task and get the work done.

★ 4. **Repulsive or filthy.**
Change 1 letter.
Have students list synonyms for *vile* (*nasty, repulsive, horrid, miserable*).

2. **An instrument or thing made for a purpose.**
Change 1 letter.

Once you've written a rough draft, you can __revise__ structure and word choice for clarity, and then ___edit___ capitalization, punctuation, and spelling to polish it for presentation!

Read each clue and write the answer in the blanks.
Use the first and last words to fill in the sentence under the ladder.

MATH

KEEP COUNTING

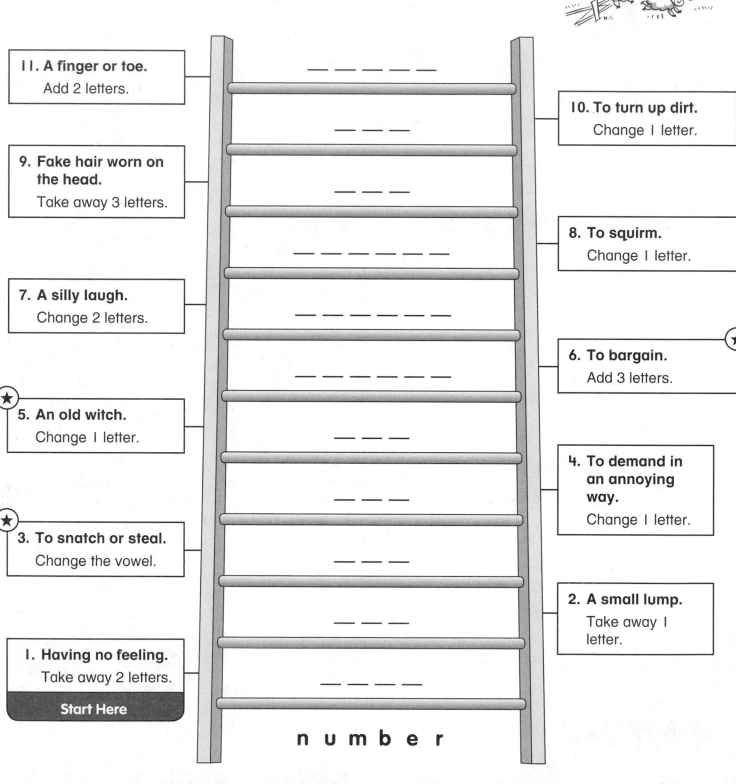

11. A finger or toe.
Add 2 letters.

10. To turn up dirt.
Change 1 letter.

9. Fake hair worn on the head.
Take away 3 letters.

8. To squirm.
Change 1 letter.

7. A silly laugh.
Change 2 letters.

6. To bargain. ★
Add 3 letters.

5. An old witch. ★
Change 1 letter.

4. To demand in an annoying way.
Change 1 letter.

3. To snatch or steal. ★
Change the vowel.

2. A small lump.
Take away 1 letter.

1. Having no feeling.
Take away 2 letters.

Start Here

n u m b e r

The _____ 28 is made up of two _____ s.

KEEP COUNTING
Answer Key and Teaching Notes

11. A finger or toe.
Add 2 letters.

d i g i t

10. To turn up dirt.
Change 1 letter.

d i g

9. Fake hair worn on the head.
Take away 3 letters.

w i g

8. To squirm.
Change 1 letter.
Have students list synonyms for *wiggle* (*jiggle, squirm, twist, writhe*).

w i g g l e

7. A silly laugh.
Change 2 letters.
Figure of speech: *for kicks and giggles,* doing something just for fun.

g i g g l e

h a g g l e

6. To bargain. ★
Add 3 letters.

★ **5. An old witch.**
Change 1 letter.

h a g

4. To demand in an annoying way.
Change 1 letter.
Multiple meaning word: an old horse.

n a g

★ **3. To snatch or steal.**
Change the vowel.

n a b

2. A small lump.
Take away 1 letter.

n u b

1. Having no feeling.
Take away 2 letters.

Start Here

n u m b

n u m b e r

The __number__ 28 is made up of two __digit__ s.

Read each clue and write the answer in the blanks.
Use the first and last words to fill in the sentence under the ladder.

MATH

WHAT'S THE TAKEAWAY?

11. To take something away.
Add 5 letters.

_ _ _ _ _ _ _ _ _ _ _

10. Our teacher was sick, so we had a ____.
Rearrange the letters.

_ _ _

9. Transports you to and from school.
Change 1 letter.

_ _ _

8. A small, round type of bread.
Change 1 letter.

_ _ _ _

★ **7. To forbid.**
Take away 1 letter.

_ _ _ _

6. I play tuba in the marching ____.
Change 1 letter.

_ _ _ _

5. To pass something to someone.
Take away 1 letter.

_ _ _ _ _

4. Good at fixing things.
Change 2 letters.

_ _ _ _ _

3. The cake had a lot of decoration, so it was very ____.
Change 2 letters.

_ _ _ _ _

2. A barrier enclosing an outdoor area.
Take away 4 letters.

_ _ _ _ _ _

★ **1. A guess based on evidence.**
Take away the first 2 letters, then add 2.

Start Here

_ _ _ _ _ _ _ _ _ _

d i f f e r e n c e

When you _____ one amount from another, the answer is called the _____.

WHAT'S THE TAKEAWAY?
Answer Key and Teaching Notes

11. To take something away.

Add 5 letters.

9. Transports you to and from school.

Change 1 letter.

Figure of speech: *throw under the bus*, to harm someone to gain advantage for yourself.

⭐ **7. To forbid.**

Take away 1 letter.

5. To pass something to someone.

Take away 1 letter.

3. The cake had a lot of decoration, so it was very _____.

Change 2 letters.

⭐ **1. A guess based on evidence.**

Take away the first 2 letters, then add 2.

Start Here

---

s u b t r a c t

s u b

b u s

b u n

b a n

b a n d

h a n d

h a n d y

f a n c y

f e n c e

i n f e r e n c e

d i f f e r e n c e

---

10. Our teacher was sick, so we had a _____.

Rearrange the letters.

Multiple meaning word: a ship that moves completely underwater.

8. A small, round type of bread.

Change 1 letter.

6. I play tuba in the marching _____.

Change 1 letter.

Have students describe the different musicians in a band (drummer, lead singer, back-up singer, guitarist).

4. Good at fixing things.

Change 2 letters.

2. A barrier enclosing an outdoor area.

Take away 4 letters.

When you ___subtract___ one amount from another, the answer is called the ___difference___.

Name _____

Read each clue and write the answer in the blanks.
Use the first and last words to fill in the sentence under the ladder.

HINT! Words with a (★) are more challenging!

MATH

MORE, MORE, MORE!

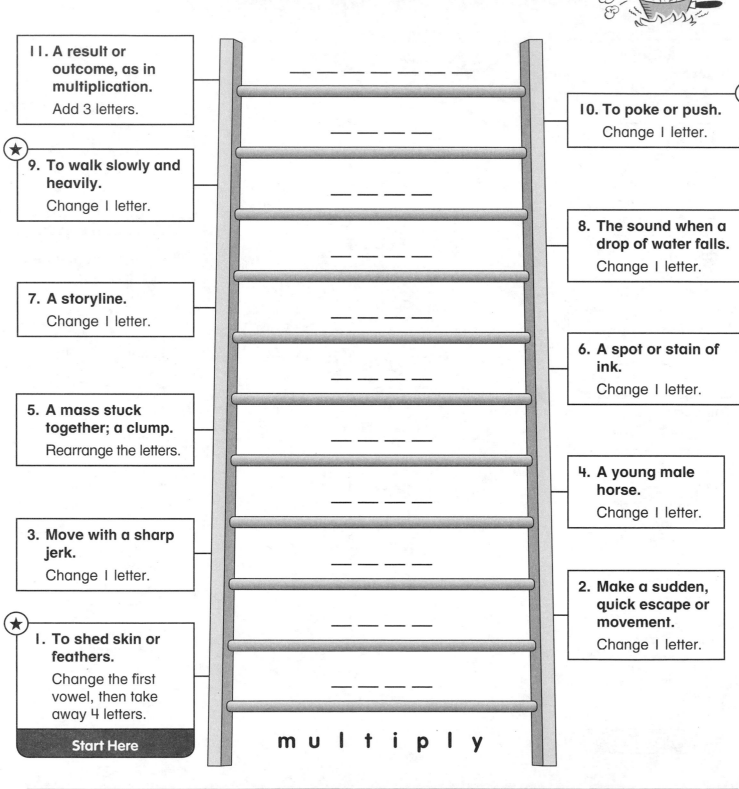

11. A result or outcome, as in multiplication.
Add 3 letters.

_ _ _ _ _ _ _

(★) 9. To walk slowly and heavily.
Change 1 letter.

_ _ _ _

7. A storyline.
Change 1 letter.

_ _ _ _

5. A mass stuck together; a clump.
Rearrange the letters.

_ _ _ _

3. Move with a sharp jerk.
Change 1 letter.

_ _ _ _

(★) 1. To shed skin or feathers.
Change the first vowel, then take away 4 letters.

Start Here

_ _ _ _

(★) 10. To poke or push.
Change 1 letter.

_ _ _ _

8. The sound when a drop of water falls.
Change 1 letter.

_ _ _ _

6. A spot or stain of ink.
Change 1 letter.

_ _ _ _

4. A young male horse.
Change 1 letter.

_ _ _ _

2. Make a sudden, quick escape or movement.
Change 1 letter.

m u l t i p l y

When you _____ two numbers, the answer is called the _____.

TIP! You may want to offer students some extra support for these more challenging words, marked with a ★.

MORE, MORE, MORE!
Answer Key and Teaching Notes

11. A result or outcome, as in multiplication.
Add 3 letters.

p r o d u c t

10. To poke or push. ★
Change 1 letter.

p r o d

★ 9. To walk slowly and heavily.
Change 1 letter.

p l o d

8. The sound when a drop of water falls.
Change 1 letter.
Have students list other onomatopoetic words, which mimic their sound (*pow, bang, fizz, boom, whoop*).

p l o p

7. A storyline.
Change 1 letter.
Have students list basic elements of a plot (character, setting, problem, obstacle, solution).

p l o t

b l o t

6. A spot or stain of ink.
Change 1 letter.

5. A mass stuck together; a clump.
Rearrange the letters.
Multiple meaning word: something your blood does so you don't keep bleeding.

c l o t

c o l t

4. A young male horse.
Change 1 letter.

3. Move with a sharp jerk.
Change 1 letter.

j o l t

b o l t

2. Make a sudden, quick escape or movement.
Change 1 letter.

★ 1. To shed skin or feathers.
Change the first vowel, then take away 4 letters.

Start Here

m o l t

m u l t i p l y

When you ___multiply___ two numbers, the answer is called the ___product___.

Name _____

Read each clue and write the answer in the blanks.
Use the first and last words to fill in the sentence under the ladder.

HINT! Words with a ★ are more challenging!

MATH

LONG DIVISION

11. A share of something.
Add 2 letters.

_ _ _ _ _ _ _

10. To separate.
Add 2 letters.

_ _ _ _ _ _

9. To jump into water head first.
Change 1 letter.

_ _ _ _

8. Where bees live.
Change 1 letter.

_ _ _ _

7. To possess or own.
Take away 1 letter.

_ _ _ _

6. To cut hair off the body in places where one doesn't want hair.
Add 1 letter.

_ _ _ _ _

5. To rescue.
Rearrange the letters.

_ _ _ _

4. A decorative container for flowers.
Change 1 letter.

_ _ _ _

3. A device used to squeeze tightly.
Take away the last 3 letters, then add 1.

_ _ _ _ _ _

2. Ability to see.
Take away the last 2 letters, then add 3.

1. A hat that protects from the sun.
Take away 2 letters.

_ _ _ _ _

Start Here

d i v i s o r

The _____ is divided by the _____ to find the quotient.

LONG DIVISION
Answer Key and Teaching Notes

11. A share of something.
Add 2 letters.

d i v i d e n d

10. To separate.
Add 2 letters.

d i v i d e

9. To jump into water head first.
Change 1 letter.

d i v e

8. Where bees live.
Change 1 letter.
Teach students that a queen bee can lay 2,500 eggs per day.

h i v e

7. To possess or own.
Take away 1 letter.

h a v e

5. To rescue.
Rearrange the letters.
In pairs, have students list things they would like to save up for.

s h a v e

6. To cut hair off the body in places where one doesn't want hair.
Add 1 letter.

s a v e

3. A device used to squeeze tightly.
Take away the last 3 letters, then add 1.

v a s e

4. A decorative container for flowers.
Change 1 letter.

v i s e

1. A hat that protects from the sun.
Take away 2 letters.

v i s i o n

2. Ability to see.
Take away the last 2 letters, then add 3.
Multiple meaning word: an idea you picture mentally of something that you want to have happen.

Start Here

v i s o r

d i v i s o r

The ___dividend___ is divided by the _____divisor_____ to find the quotient.

Read each clue and write the answer in the blanks.
Use the first and last words to fill in the sentence under the ladder.

DIVVY UP

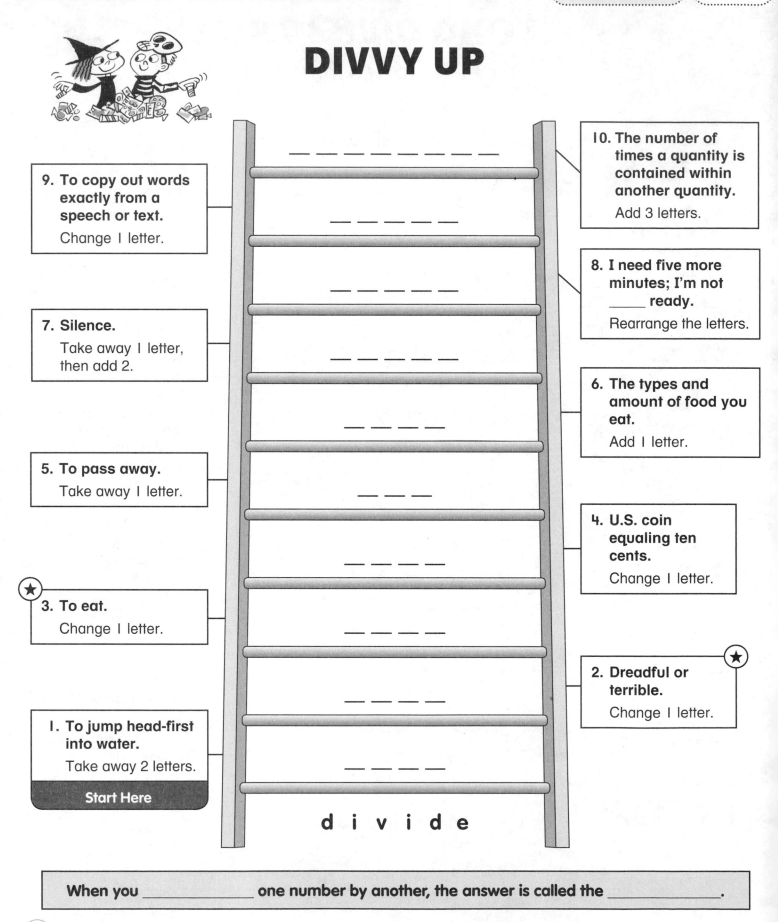

9. To copy out words exactly from a speech or text.

Change 1 letter.

7. Silence.

Take away 1 letter, then add 2.

5. To pass away.

Take away 1 letter.

★ **3.** To eat.

Change 1 letter.

1. To jump head-first into water.

Take away 2 letters.

Start Here

10. The number of times a quantity is contained within another quantity.

Add 3 letters.

8. I need five more minutes; I'm not _____ ready.

Rearrange the letters.

6. The types and amount of food you eat.

Add 1 letter.

4. U.S. coin equaling ten cents.

Change 1 letter.

★ **2.** Dreadful or terrible.

Change 1 letter.

d i v i d e

When you _____ one number by another, the answer is called the _____.

DIVVY UP
Answer Key and Teaching Notes

q u o t i e n t

q u o t e

q u i t e

q u i e t

d i e t

d i e

d i m e

d i n e

d i r e

d i v e

d i v i d e

Start Here

---

9. To copy out words exactly from a speech or text.

Change 1 letter.

7. Silence.

Take away 1 letter, then add 2.

Have students list synonyms for *quiet* (*soft, muted, low, muffled*).

5. To pass away.

Take away 1 letter.

★ **3. To eat.**

Change 1 letter.

In pairs, have students share, "My favorite place to dine is….."

1. To jump head-first into water.
Take away 2 letters.

---

10. The number of times a quantity is contained within another quantity.

Add 3 letters.

8. I need five more minutes; I'm not _____ ready.

Rearrange the letters.

6. The types and amount of food you eat.

Add 1 letter.

4. U.S. coin equaling ten cents.

Change 1 letter.

★ **2. Dreadful or terrible.**

Change 1 letter.

Figure of speech: *in dire straits*, in a very bad situation.

When you ____**divide**____ one number by another, the answer is called the ____**quotient**____.

Name _____

Read each clue and write the answer in the blanks.
Use the first and last words to fill in the sentence under the ladder.

MATH

ABOVE & BELOW

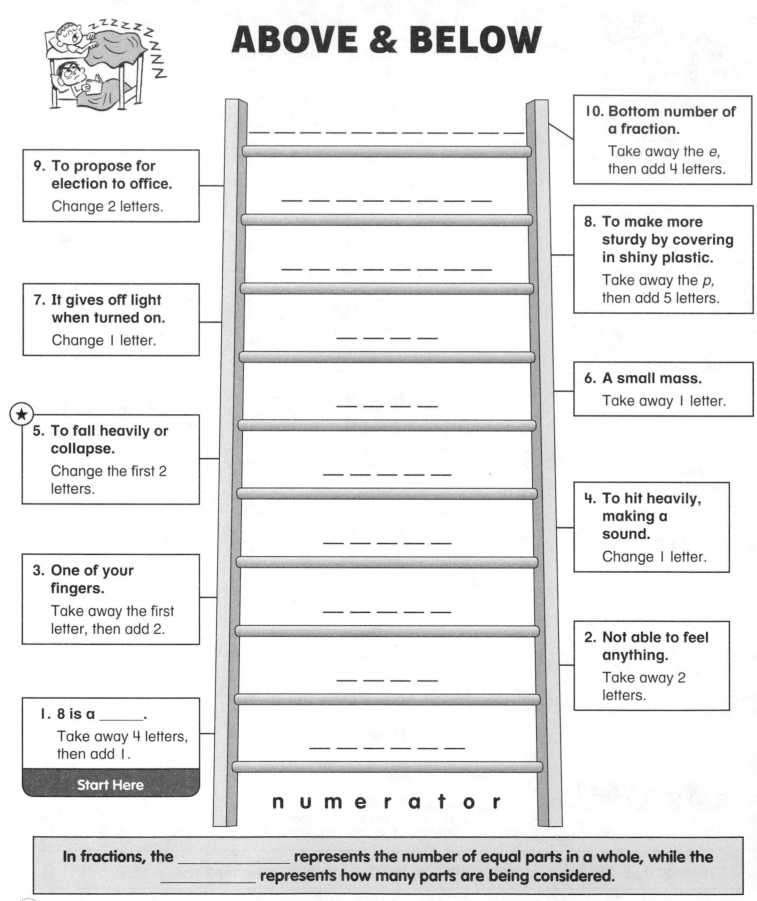

9. To propose for election to office.
Change 2 letters.

7. It gives off light when turned on.
Change 1 letter.

★ 5. To fall heavily or collapse.
Change the first 2 letters.

3. One of your fingers.
Take away the first letter, then add 2.

1. 8 is a _____.
Take away 4 letters, then add 1.

Start Here

10. Bottom number of a fraction.
Take away the *e*, then add 4 letters.

8. To make more sturdy by covering in shiny plastic.
Take away the *p*, then add 5 letters.

6. A small mass.
Take away 1 letter.

4. To hit heavily, making a sound.
Change 1 letter.

2. Not able to feel anything.
Take away 2 letters.

n u m e r a t o r

In fractions, the _____ represents the number of equal parts in a whole, while the _____ represents how many parts are being considered.

TIP! You may want to offer students some extra support for these more challenging words, marked with a ★.

ABOVE & BELOW
Answer Key and Teaching Notes

d e n o m i n a t o r

10. Bottom number of a fraction.
Take away the *e*, then add 4 letters.

9. To propose for election to office.
Change 2 letters.

n o m i n a t e

l a m i n a t e

8. To make more sturdy by covering in shiny plastic.
Take away the *p*, then add 5 letters.

7. It gives off light when turned on.
Change 1 letter.

l a m p

l u m p

6. A small mass.
Take away 1 letter.

★ **5. To fall heavily or collapse.**
Change the first 2 letters.

Multiple meaning word: when you feel down or don't perform well. Have a couple students share a time they were "in a slump."

s l u m p

t h u m p

4. To hit heavily, making a sound.
Change 1 letter.

t h u m b

3. One of your fingers.
Take away the first letter, then add 2.

2. Not able to feel anything.
Take away 2 letters. Have students name a time when they might feel physically numb (being inside a freezer).

n u m b

1. 8 is a _____.
Take away 4 letters, then add 1.

Start Here

n u m b e r

n u m e r a t o r

In fractions, the __denominator__ represents the number of equal parts in a whole, while the __numerator__ represents how many parts are being considered.

Name _____

Read each clue and write the answer in the blanks.
Use the first and last words to fill in the sentence under the ladder.

HINT! Words with a (★) are more challenging!

MATH

RAISED UP

11. Superman has the ____ of flight.
Change 1 letter.

— — — — —

10. To crouch in fear. ★
Change 1 letter.

9. A widow's share of her husband's estate. ★
Change 1 letter.

— — — — —

8. Antonym of *higher*.
Change 1 letter.

— — — — —

7. A person who doesn't *win*.
Take away 1 letter, then add 2.

— — — — —

6. When something is missing, it is ____.
Change 1 letter.

— — — — —

5. Antonym of *win*.
Change 1 letter.

— — — —

4. A recommended quantity of medicine.
Change 1 letter.

— — — —

3. To raise a question.
Take away 2 letters.

— — — —

2. To uncover. ★
Add 2 letters.

— — — — — —

1. An exhibition or show.
Take away 4 letters.

Start Here

— — — —

e x p o n e n t

The _____ represents the _____ to which a number or expression is raised.

RAISED UP
Answer Key and Teaching Notes

11. Superman has the ____ of flight.
Change 1 letter.

★ 9. A widow's share of her husband's estate.
Change 1 letter.

7. A person who doesn't *win*.
Take away 1 letter, then add 2.

5. Antonym of *win*.
Change 1 letter.
Discuss the different pronunciations of *-ose*, as in *lose* and *dose*.

3. To raise a question.
Take away 2 letters.

1. An exhibition or show.
Take away 4 letters.

Start Here

p o w e r

c o w e r

d o w e r

l o w e r

l o s e r

l o s t

l o s e

d o s e

p o s e

e x p o s e

e x p o

e x p o n e n t

★ 10. To crouch in fear.
Change 1 letter.
In pairs, have students start and finish the sentence, "I would cower if …."

8. Antonym of *higher*.
Change 1 letter.

6. When something is missing, it is ____.
Change 1 letter.

4. A recommended quantity of medicine.
Change 1 letter.

★ 2. To uncover.
Add 2 letters.
Teach students that an *exposé* is a shocking report or discovery of facts.

The __exponent__ represents the __power__ to which a number or expression is raised.

Name _____

Read each clue and write the answer in the blanks.
Use the first and last words to fill in the sentence under the ladder.

HINT! Words with a (★) are more challenging!

MATH

SUPERPOWERS

11. Salary was a _____ in my decision to change jobs.
Add 2 letters.

— — — — — — —

10. A known truth.
Change 1 letter.

— — — — —

9. Front part of the head.
Change 2 letters.

— — — —

8. Antonym of *early*.
Take away 1 letter, then add 2.

— — — —

7. A place equipped for scientific experimentation or research.
Take away 1 letter.

— — —

6. A baby sheep.
Change the first vowel, then take away 2 letters.

— — — —

(★) 5. Wood.
Take away 1 letter.

— — — — — — —

4. To sleep.
Change 1 letter.

— — — — — — — —

3. You call this person to fix a water leak.
Add 3 letters.

— — — — — — —

2. A purple fruit.
Take away 1 letter.

— — — —

(★) 1. A column of smoke.
Take away 3 letters (*i, l, t*), then rearrange.

— — — — —

Start Here

m u l t i p l e

You multiply _____s to get an answer; the answer is a _____ of the numbers you multiplied.

TM ® & © Scholastic Inc. All rights reserved. *Daily Word Ladders* copyright © 2019 by Timothy V. Rasinski and Melissa Cheesman Smith. Published by Scholastic Inc.

SUPERPOWERS
Answer Key and Teaching Notes

f a c t o r

11. Salary was a _____ in my decision to change jobs.
Add 2 letters.

10. A known truth.
Change 1 letter.

f a c t

f a c e

9. Front part of the head.
Change 2 letters.
Multiple meaning word: to deal with.

8. Antonym of *early*.
Take away 1 letter, then add 2.
Have students list places where they shouldn't arrive late (school, doctor's appointment).

l a t e

l a b

7. A place equipped for scientific experimentation or research.
Take away 1 letter.

l a m b

6. A baby sheep.
Change the first vowel, then take away 2 letters.
Figure of speech: *in two shakes of a lamb's tail,* a short amount of time.

★
5. Wood.
Take away 1 letter.

l u m b e r

s l u m b e r

3. You call this person to fix a water leak.
Add 3 letters.

p l u m b e r

4. To sleep.
Change 1 letter.

p l u m

★
1. A column of smoke.
Take away 3 letters (*i, l, t*), then rearrange.

Start Here

p l u m e

2. A purple fruit.
Take away 1 letter.

m u l t i p l e

You multiply __factor__s to get an answer; the answer is a __multiple__ of the numbers you multiplied.

Read each clue and write the answer in the blanks.
Use the first and last words to fill in the sentence under the ladder.

MATH

FACTOR IT IN

11. A combination of things.
Add 2 letters.

— — — — — — — — —

10. To create a piece of music.
Change 1 letter.

— — — — — — — —

★ **9. A mixture of substances used to fertilize soil.**
Add 3 letters.

— — — — — — — —

8. A strong, sturdy piece of wood at the end of a fence.
Rearrange the letters.

— — — — —

7. To end or finish.
Add 1 letter.

— — — — —

6. Opposite of *bottom*.
Change 1 letter.

— — — —

5. A clue or a piece of information.
Take away 1 letter.

— — —

4. A vacation.
Change 1 letter.

— — — —

3. To remove something by cutting it.
Change 1 letter.

— — — — —

2. The flat band on a hat.
Change 1 letter.

— — — —

★ **1. Proper and formal.**
Take away 1 letter.

Start Here

— — — —

p r i m e

A _____ number can only be divided by itself and 1, while a _____ can be divided by multiple numbers.

FACTOR IT IN
Answer Key and Teaching Notes

11. A combination of things.

Add 2 letters.

Have students determine the number of syllables (vowel sounds) in the word.

c o m p o s i t e

10. To create a piece of music.

Change 1 letter.

c o m p o s e

★ **9. A mixture of substances used to fertilize soil.**

Add 3 letters.

c o m p o s t

8. A strong, sturdy piece of wood at the end of a fence.

Rearrange the letters.

p o s t

7. To end or finish.

Add 1 letter.

s t o p

5. A clue or a piece of information.

Take away 1 letter.

Multiple meaning word: extra money given to a waiter for his service, typically 15 to 20 percent of the bill.

t o p

6. Opposite of *bottom*.

Change 1 letter.

t i p

4. A vacation.

Change 1 letter.

Multiple meaning word: *stumble*.

t r i p

3. To remove something by cutting it.

Change 1 letter.

t r i m

2. The flat band on a hat.

Change 1 letter.

b r i m

★ **1. Proper and formal.**

Take away 1 letter.

Start Here

p r i m

p r i m e

A __prime__ number can only be divided by itself and 1, while a __composite__ number can be divided by multiple numbers.

Name _____

Read each clue and write the answer in the blanks.
Use the first and last words to fill in the sentence under the ladder.

MATH

MORE THAN AVERAGE

11. My preferred ____ of travel is by plane.

Change 1 letter.

9. To deal with a difficulty.

Change 1 letter.

7. When fruit is ready to eat.

Add 1 letter.

5. The edge of a bowl or cup.

Change 1 letter.

(★) 3. A female horse.

Change 1 letter.

1. Lunch or dinner.

Change 1 letter.

Start Here

— — — —

— — — —

— — — —

— — — —

— — — —

— — —

— — —

— — —

— — — —

— — — —

— — — —

m e a n

10. A system for communicating, such as on a telegraph.

Change 1 letter.

8. A strong, thick cord.

Change 1 letter.

6. To tear up.

Change 1 letter.

4. To run into something with force.

Take away 1 letter, then rearrange the remaining letters.

2. Antonym of *female*.

Rearrange the letters.

A _____ is the average of a set of numbers, while the _____ is the most common or frequent number of the set.

TIP! You may want to offer students some extra support for these more challenging words, marked with a ★.

MORE THAN AVERAGE
Answer Key and Teaching Notes

m o d e

c o d e

c o p e

r o p e

r i p e

r i p

r i m

r a m

m a r e

m a l e

m e a l

m e a n

11. My preferred ____ of travel is by plane.
Change 1 letter.

9. To deal with a difficulty.
Change 1 letter.
In pairs, have students describe a time when they had to cope with something difficult.

7. When fruit is ready to eat.
Add 1 letter.

5. The edge of a bowl or cup.
Change 1 letter.

★
3. A female horse.
Change 1 letter.

1. Lunch or dinner.
Change 1 letter.
Start Here

10. A system for communicating, such as on a telegraph.
Change 1 letter.

8. A strong, thick cord.
Change 1 letter.
Figure of speech: *rope someone in*, to persuade someone to do something.

6. To tear up.
Change 1 letter.

4. To run into something with force.
Take away 1 letter, then rearrange the remaining letters.

2. Antonym of *female*.
Rearrange the letters.
Homophone: *mail*, something delivered by the post office.

A _____ **mean** _____ is the average of a set of numbers, while the _____ **mode** _____ is the most common or frequent number of the set.

Read each clue and write the answer in the blanks.
Use the first and last words to fill in the sentence under the ladder.

HINT! Words with a (★) are more challenging!

MATH

LINE IT UP

11. Can be right, obtuse, or acute.
Rearrange the letters.

_ _ _ _ _

10. Antonym of *devil*.
Change 1 letter.

_ _ _ _ _

9. Feeling mad.
Take away 1 letter.

_ _ _ _ _

8. I put my coat on the _____ in the closet.
Change 1 letter.

_ _ _ _ _ _

7. The possibility of harm.
Change 1 letter.

_ _ _ _ _

6. A slang word for a *home run* in baseball.
Change 1 letter. (★)

_ _ _ _ _ _

5. To stay somewhere longer than normal. (★)
Take away 1 letter, then add 2.

_ _ _ _ _

4. Something shiny and sparkly.
Change 1 letter.

_ _ _ _ _

3. Unable to see.
Change 1 letter.

_ _ _ _ _

2. Quickly closing and opening both eyes.
Add 1 letter.

_ _ _ _

1. A small part of a longer chain.
Change 1 letter.

Start Here

l i n e

A _____ has an _____ of 180 degrees.

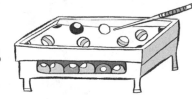

TIP! You may want to offer students some extra support for these more challenging words, marked with a ⊛.

LINE IT UP
Answer Key and Teaching Notes

11. Can be right, obtuse, or acute.

Rearrange the letters.

Teach students that a straight angle is one that is 180 degrees and can also be called a *line* or *line segment*.

9. Feeling mad.

Take away 1 letter.

7. The possibility of harm.

Change 1 letter.

⊛ **5. To stay somewhere longer than normal.**

Take away 1 letter, then add 2.

3. Unable to see.

Change 1 letter.

1. A small part of a longer chain.

Change 1 letter.

Start Here

a n g l e

a n g e l

a n g e r

h a n g e r

d a n g e r

d i n g e r

l i n g e r

b l i n g

b l i n d

b l i n k

l i n k

l i n e

10. Antonym of *devil*.

Change 1 letter.

Have students point out and notice the differences between the spellings of *angel* and *angle*.

8. I put my coat on the _____ in the closet.

Change 1 letter.

Homophone: *hangar*, a building used to hold an airplane.

⊛ **6. A slang word for a *home run* in baseball.**

Change 1 letter.

4. Something shiny and sparkly.

Change 1 letter.

2. Quickly closing and opening both eyes.

Add 1 letter.

A ___line___ has an ___angle___ of 180 degrees.

Name _____

Read each clue and write the answer in the blanks.
Use the first and last words to fill in the sentence under the ladder.

MATH

UP, DOWN & ACROSS

11. **Parallel to level ground.**
    Add 3 letters.

10. **Where land meets sky.**
    Take away the last letter, then add 4.

9. **A designated area sometimes shown with cones.**
    Change 1 letter.

8. **The construction was marked with an orange ____.**
    Change 1 letter.

★ 7. **Used with the word *out*; to fall asleep.**
    Change 1 letter.

★ 6. **A member of a monastery.**
    Change 2 letters.

5. **A drink that comes from a cow.**
    Change 1 letter.

4. **To grind a grain.**
    Change 1 letter.

3. **A plant used for flavoring food, such as pickles.**
    Change 1 letter.

2. **I tried to ____ the phone number multiple times.**
    Change 1 letter.

★ 1. **A small glass container to hold liquids.**
    Take away 4 letters.

Start Here

v e r t i c a l

A _____ line goes side to side, or across, while a _____ line goes up and down.

UP, DOWN & ACROSS
Answer Key and Teaching Notes

h o r i z o n t a l

h o r i z o n

z o n e

c o n e

c o n k

m o n k

m i l k

m i l l

d i l l

d i a l

v i a l

v e r t i c a l

11. Parallel to level ground.

Add 3 letters.

Show students what *horizontal* and *vertical* look like using your arms.

9. A designated area sometimes shown with cones.

Change 1 letter.

★ **7. Used with the word *out*; to fall asleep.**

Change 1 letter.

5. A drink that comes from a cow.

Change 1 letter.

3. A plant used for flavoring food, such as pickles.

Change 1 letter.

★ **1. A small glass container to hold liquids.**

Take away 4 letters.

Start Here

10. Where land meets sky.

Take away the last letter, then add 4.

Show students digital images of the horizon.

8. The construction was marked with an orange _____.

Change 1 letter.

★ **6. A member of a monastery.**

Change 2 letters.

4. To grind a grain.

Change 1 letter.

Figure of speech: *rumor mill*, a system of people talking or gossiping about others.

2. I tried to _____ the phone number multiple times.

Change 1 letter.

A ___horizontal___ line goes side to side, or across, while a ___vertical___ line goes up and down.

Read each clue and write the answer in the blanks.
Use the first and last words to fill in the sentence under the ladder.

MATH

FENCED-IN

11. A designated space.
Add 1 letter.

9. A large version of a rabbit.
Change 1 letter.

★ 7. A manufactured article or product.
Change 1 letter.

5. I love to _____ books.
Change 1 letter.

★ 3. To harvest or gather.
Rearrange the letters.

1. To look closely at something.
Take away 5 letters.

Start Here

_ _ _ _ _

_ _ _

_ _ _ _

_ _ _ _ _

_ _ _ _ _

_ _ _ _

_ _ _ _

_ _ _ _

_ _ _ _

_ _ _ _

10. You _____ what you eat.
Take away 1 letter.

8. Unusual or uncommon.
Change 1 letter.

6. Truth or _____?
Rearrange the letters.

4. Antonym of *fake.*
Change 1 letter.

2. A soft fruit with yellow, green, red, or brown skin.
Change 1 letter.

p e r i m e t e r

The _____ measures the outside of a shape, while the _____ measures the space inside.

TIP! You may want to offer students some extra support for these more challenging words, marked with a ★.

FENCED-IN
Answer Key and Teaching Notes

11. A designated space.
Add 1 letter.

9. A large version of a rabbit.
Change 1 letter.

★ **7. A manufactured article or product.**
Change 1 letter.

5. I love to _____ books.
Change 1 letter.

★ **3. To harvest or gather.**
Rearrange the letters.
Figure of speech: *the grim reaper*, the personification of death.

1. To look closely at something.
Take away 5 letters.
Multiple meaning word: a person of equal standing.

Start Here

a r e a

a r e

h a r e

r a r e

w a r e

d a r e

r e a d

r e a l

r e a p

p e a r

p e e r

p e r i m e t e r

10. You ____ what you eat.
Take away 1 letter.

8. Unusual or uncommon.
Change 1 letter.

6. Truth or _____?
Rearrange the letters.

4. Antonym of *fake*.
Change 1 letter.
Homophone: *reel*, a cylinder that turns to wind something up.

2. A soft fruit with yellow, green, red, or brown skin.
Change 1 letter.

The __perimeter__ measures the outside of a shape, while the __area__ measures the space inside.

Name _____

Read each clue and write the answer in the blanks.
Use the first and last words to fill in the sentence under the ladder.

HINT! Words with a (★) are more challenging!

MATH

THE RIGHT ANGLES

11. An angle smaller than 90 degrees.

Add 1 letter.

10. A little puppy is described as ____.

Change 1 letter.

9. Silent.

Change 1 letter.

8. The baby of a horse and a donkey.

Change 1 letter, then rearrange the letters.

7. Another name for gas in a car.

Take away the *s*, then add 1 letter to the end.

6. To join together to form a single unit. (★)

Take away 2 letters.

5. To indicate that you will not do something.

Add 1 letter.

4. To use again.

Change 2 letters.

3. To entertain.

Change 2 letters.

2. To stop for a short time.

Add 2 letters.

1. You can ___ a pen to write.

Take away 3 letters.

Start Here

o b t u s e

An _____ angle is greater than 90 degrees, while an _____ angle is less than 90 degrees.

76

TM ® & © Scholastic Inc. All rights reserved. *Daily Word Ladders* copyright © 2019 by Timothy V. Rasinski and Melissa Cheesman Smith. Published by Scholastic In

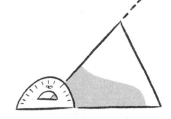

THE RIGHT ANGLES
Answer Key and Teaching Notes

11. An angle smaller than 90 degrees.

Add 1 letter.

Have students make acute and obtuse angles with their hands.

9. Silent.

Change 1 letter.

7. Another name for gas in a car.

Take away the *s*, then add 1 letter to the end.

5. To indicate that you will not do something.

Add 1 letter.

Homograph: (noun) something that is thrown away.

3. To entertain.

Change 2 letters.

1. You can ___ a pen to write.

Take away 3 letters.

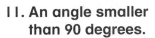
Start Here

a c u t e

c u t e

m u t e

m u l e

f u e l

f u s e

r e f u s e

r e u s e

a m u s e

p a u s e

u s e

o b t u s e

10. A little puppy is described as ___.

Change 1 letter.

8. The baby of a horse and a donkey.

Change 1 letter, then rearrange the letters.

(★)

6. To join together to form a single unit.

Take away 2 letters.

4. To use again.

Change 2 letters.

Have students list the words that may be used with *reuse* when talking about how to save the planet (*reduce, recycle*).

2. To stop for a short time.

Add 2 letters.

An _____**obtuse**_____ angle is greater than 90 degrees, while an _____**acute**_____ angle is less than 90 degrees.

Name _____

Read each clue and write the answer in the blanks.
Use the first and last words to fill in the sentence under the ladder.

HINT! Words with a (★) are more challenging!

MATH

WE LOVE TRIANGLES

11. A triangle with sides of different lengths.
Add 2 letters.

— — — — — — — —

10. Used to measure weight.
Change 1 letter.

— — — — — —

9. The skin that covers your skull.
Add 2 letters.

— — — — — —

8. The fluid inside of a tree.
Change 1 letter.

— — — —

7. To droop down.
Take away 1 letter.

— — — —

★

6. A wise person.
Take away 1 letter.

— — — —

5. A platform used for performance.
Change 1 letter.

— — — — —

4. A stick used to support a plant.
Change 1 letter.

— — — — —

3. Old and dried out.
Add 1 letter.

— — — — —

2. My favorite store has a 50%-off ____.
Change 1 letter.

— — — —

1. The only one.
Take away 5 letters.

Start Here

— — — —

i s o s c e l e s

The sides of a _____ triangle are all different lengths, while an _____ triangle has two sides of the same length.

WE LOVE TRIANGLES
Answer Key and Teaching Notes

11. A triangle with sides of different lengths.
Add 2 letters.

s c a l e n e

10. Used to measure weight.
Change 1 letter.

s c a l e

9. The skin that covers your skull.
Add 2 letters.

s c a l p

8. The fluid inside of a tree.
Change 1 letter.

s a p

7. To droop down.
Take away 1 letter.

s a g

6. A wise person. ★
Take away 1 letter.

s a g e

5. A platform used for performance.
Change 1 letter.
Multiple meaning word: one part or phase of a process.

s t a g e

4. A stick used to support a plant.
Change 1 letter.

s t a k e

s t a l e

3. Old and dried out.
Add 1 letter.

s a l e

2. My favorite store has a 50%-off ____.
Change 1 letter.
Homophone: *sail*, a part of a boat.

s o l e

1. The only one.
Take away 5 letters.

Start Here

i s o s c e l e s

The sides of a ___scalene___ triangle are all different lengths, while an ___isosceles___ triangle has two sides of the same length.

Read each clue and write the answer in the blanks.
Use the first and last words to fill in the sentence under the ladder.

HINT! Words with a ★ are more challenging!

MATH

STRIKE A CHORD

11. A round shape.
Take away 1 letter, then add 2.

— — — — — —

10. A repeated series of occurrences.
Take away 2 letters.

— — — — — —

9. A tornado.
Add 2 letters.

— — — — — — —

8. An exact copy. ★
Add 1 letter.

— — — — —

7. I got my ice cream in a ____.
Change 1 letter.

— — — —

6. To handle.
Change 1 letter.

— — — —

5. To look forward to.
Change 1 letter.

— — — —

4. To sharpen or perfect. ★
Add 1 letter.

— — — —

3. 6 x 2 – 11 = ___
Change 1 letter.

— — —

2. A metal-bearing rock.
Take away 2 letters.

— — —

1. My ____ at home is to take out the garbage.
Change 1 letter.

Start Here

— — — — —

c h o r d

A line called a _____ touches any two outside points of a _____.

STRIKE A CHORD
Answer Key and Teaching Notes

11. A round shape.
Take away 1 letter, then add 2.

9. A tornado.
Add 2 letters.
Have students count the number of syllables (vowel sounds) in the word.

7. I got my ice cream in a ____.
Change 1 letter.

5. To look forward to.
Change 1 letter.

3. 6 x 2 – 11 = ___
Change 1 letter.

1. My ____ at home is to take out the garbage.
Change 1 letter.

Start Here

10. A repeated series of occurrences.
Take away 2 letters.
Discuss with students the commonly taught cycle of the butterfly (*egg, caterpillar, chrysalis, butterfly*).

8. An exact copy. ★
Add 1 letter.

6. To handle.
Change 1 letter.

4. To sharpen or perfect. ★
Add 1 letter.

2. A metal-bearing rock.
Take away 2 letters.
Homophone: *or*, a conjunction used to connect two things.

Ladder (bottom to top):
c h o r d
c h o r e
o r e
o n e
h o n e
h o p e
c o p e
c o n e
c l o n e
c y c l o n e
c y c l e
c i r c l e

TIP! You may want to offer students some extra support for these more challenging words, marked with a ★.

A line called a ___chord___ touches any two outside points of a ___circle___.

Name _____

Read each clue and write the answer in the blanks.
Use the first and last words to fill in the sentence under the ladder.

PIZZA PIE

11. The width of a circle or sphere.
Add 3 letters.

— — — — — — — — —

10. Measurements of beats in music.
Add 1 letter, then rearrange.

— — — — —

9. To join together.
Change 1 letter.

— — — —

8. Vegetarians don't eat _____.
Rearrange the letters.

— — — —

7. An organized group in sports.
Change 1 letter.

— — — — —

6. A railcar in a mine.
Take away the last 2 letters, then add 1.

— — — — — —

5. To teach a skill.
Change 1 letter.

— — — — —

4. Where emotions and intellect exist.
Change 1 letter.

— — — — —

3. To empty liquid.
Add 1 letter, then rearrange.

— — — —

1. The song was playing loudly on the _____.
Take away the last 2 letters, then add 1.

Start Here

— — — —

2. A sudden attack on an enemy.
Take away the last letter, then rearrange the remaining letters.

r a d i u s

The _____ extends from any point on a circle's perimeter to its center. Extending this line to the other side of the circle gives you the _____.

PIZZA PIE
Answer Key and Teaching Notes

11. The width of a circle or sphere.

Add 3 letters.

Show students how the diameter is also a *chord*, a straight line touching two points of the edge of the circle, but that the diameter passes through the center of the circle.

9. To join together.
Change 1 letter.

7. An organized group in sports.
Change 1 letter.

5. To teach a skill.
Change 1 letter.

3. To empty liquid.
Add 1 letter, then rearrange.

1. The song was playing loudly on the _____.
Take away the last 2 letters, then add 1.

Start Here

10. Measurements of beats in music.
Add 1 letter, then rearrange.

8. Vegetarians don't eat _____.
Rearrange the letters.

6. A railcar in a mine. ★
Take away the last 2 letters, then add 1.

4. Where emotions and intellect exist.
Change 1 letter.
Figure of speech: *get your brain in gear*, to start thinking.

2. A sudden attack on an enemy.
Take away the last letter, then rearrange the remaining letters.

Ladder (top to bottom):

d i a m e t e r

m e t e r

m e e t

m e a t

t e a m

t r a m

t r a i n

b r a i n

d r a i n

r a i d

r a d i o

r a d i u s

The __radius__ extends from any point on a circle's perimeter to its center. Extending this line to the other side of the circle gives you the __diameter__.

83

Name _____

Read each clue and write the answer in the blanks.
Use the first and last words to fill in the sentence under the ladder.

HINT! Words with a ★ are more challenging!

MATH

YARD WORK

11. A distance of 5,280 feet.
Change 1 letter.

9. To think something over in one's mind.
Change 1 letter.

★ 7. Extra weight.
Change 1 letter.

5. The outer layer of a tree.
Change 1 letter.

3. Utensil with tines.
Change the first and last letters.

1. You may make a birthday ___ for a friend.
Take away the last letter, then change 1 letter.

Start Here

10. A hybrid of a donkey and a horse.
Change 1 letter.

8. A male cow.
Change 1 letter.

★ 6. To resist or refuse.
Change 1 letter.

4. An outdoor area for recreation.
Change 2 letters.

2. In an apple, the seeds are in the ____.
Change 2 letters.

_ _ _ _
_ _ _ _
_ _ _ _
_ _ _ _
_ _ _ _
_ _ _ _
_ _ _ _
_ _ _ _
_ _ _ _
_ _ _ _

y a r d s

There are 1,760 _____ in a _____.

YARD WORK
Answer Key and Teaching Notes

11. A distance of 5,280 feet.
Change 1 letter.

9. To think something over in one's mind.
Change 1 letter.

⭐ **7. Extra weight.**
Change 1 letter.
Teach students the meaning of *buy in bulk,* to buy a lot of something at a time.

5. The outer layer of a tree.
Change 1 letter.

3. Utensil with tines.
Change the first and last letters.

1. You may make a birthday ___ for a friend.
Take away the last letter, change 1 letter.

Start Here

m i l e

m u l e

m u l l

b u l l

b u l k

b a l k

b a r k

p a r k

f o r k

c o r e

c a r d

y a r d s

10. A hybrid of a donkey and a horse.
Change 1 letter.

8. A male cow.
Change 1 letter.
Figure of speech: *bull in a china shop,* someone who is clumsy and might break things.

⭐ **6. To resist or refuse.**
Change 1 letter.

4. An outdoor area for recreation.
Change 2 letters.
Multiple meaning word: what you do with a car when you are done driving it.

2. In an apple, the seeds are in the ___.
Change 2 letters.

There are 1,760 ____yards____ in a ____mile____.

Name _____

Read each clue and write the answer in the blanks.
Use the first and last words to fill in the sentence under the ladder.

HINT! Words with a (★) are more challenging!

MATH

WHAT'S THE METER?

11. **To cling or adhere.**
Change 1 letter.

10. **Unable to move or change.**
Change 1 letter.

9. **To pile on top of another.**
Change 1 letter.

8. **A simple wood hut.**
Change 1 letter.

7. **Lower part of the leg.**
Change 1 letter.

6. **A sea animal with sharp teeth.**
Change 1 letter.

(★) 5. **Harsh or grim.**
Change 1 letter.

4. **Opposite of *finish*.**
Change *ee* to *a*, then rearrange the letters.

3. **A road.**
Take away the first 2 letters, then add 3.

2. **The sound a bird might make.**
Take away 2 letters, then add 1.

(★) 1. **To go back and forth.**
Change the first letter, then add 1.

Start Here

m e t e r

A _____ _____ has 100 centimeters on it, and 1,000 millimeters!

TIP! You may want to offer students some extra support for these more challenging words, marked with a (★).

WHAT'S THE METER?
Answer Key and Teaching Notes

11. To cling or adhere.

Change 1 letter.

9. To pile on top of another.

Change 1 letter.

Figure of speech: *the cards were stacked against him*, someone who went into an unfair situation.

7. Lower part of the leg.

Change 1 letter.

★ 5. Harsh or grim.

Change 1 letter.

Discuss what a stark landscape looks like.

3. A road.

Take away the first 2 letters, then add 3.

★ 1. To go back and forth.

Change the first letter, then add 1.

Start Here

s t i c k

s t u c k

s t a c k

s h a c k

s h a n k

s h a r k

s t a r k

s t a r t

s t r e e t

t w e e t

t e e t e r

m e t e r

10. Unable to move or change.

Change 1 letter.

8. A simple wood hut.

Change 1 letter.

6. A sea animal with sharp teeth.

Change 1 letter.

Multiple meaning word: a crafty person who profits by taking advantage of people.

4. Opposite of *finish*.

Change *ee* to *a*, then rearrange the letters.

Have students list synonyms for *start* (*begin, kickoff, open, commence*).

2. The sound a bird might make.

Take away 2 letters, then add 1.

A ____meter____ ____stick____ has 100 centimeters on it, and 1,000 millimeters!

Name _____

Read each clue and write the answer in the blanks.
Use the first and last words to fill in the sentence under the ladder.

MATH

JUST HOW MUCH?

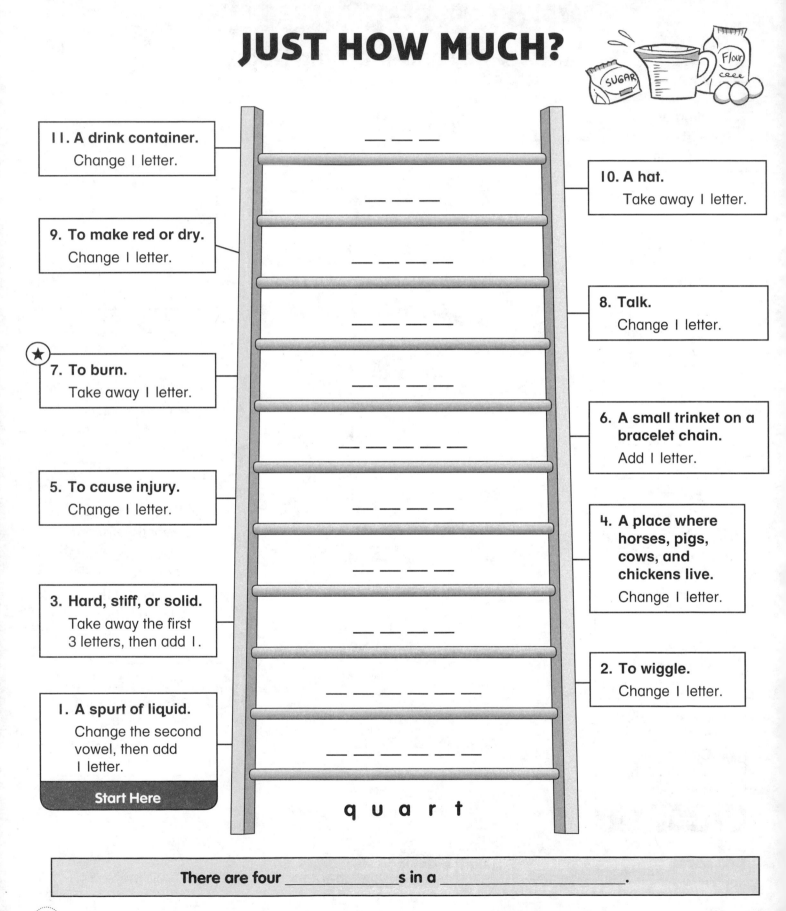

11. **A drink container.**
Change 1 letter.

9. **To make red or dry.**
Change 1 letter.

★ 7. **To burn.**
Take away 1 letter.

5. **To cause injury.**
Change 1 letter.

3. **Hard, stiff, or solid.**
Take away the first 3 letters, then add 1.

1. **A spurt of liquid.**
Change the second vowel, then add 1 letter.

Start Here

10. **A hat.**
Take away 1 letter.

8. **Talk.**
Change 1 letter.

6. **A small trinket on a bracelet chain.**
Add 1 letter.

4. **A place where horses, pigs, cows, and chickens live.**
Change 1 letter.

2. **To wiggle.**
Change 1 letter.

q u a r t

There are four _____ s in a _____.

JUST HOW MUCH?
Answer Key and Teaching Notes

11. A drink container.
Change 1 letter.

c u p

10. A hat.
Take away 1 letter.

c a p

9. To make red or dry.
Change 1 letter.
Multiple meaning word: a man.

c h a p

8. Talk.
Change 1 letter.
Have students list synonyms for *chat* (*converse, gab, yak*).

c h a t

★ **7. To burn.**
Take away 1 letter.

c h a r

5. To cause injury.
Change 1 letter.

c h a r m

6. A small trinket on a bracelet chain.
Add 1 letter.

h a r m

3. Hard, stiff, or solid.
Take away the first 3 letters, then add 1.
Multiple meaning word: a partnership that does business, like a law firm.

f a r m

4. A place where horses, pigs, cows, and chickens live.
Change 1 letter.

f i r m

s q u i r m

2. To wiggle.
Change 1 letter.

1. A spurt of liquid.
Change the second vowel, then add 1 letter.

s q u i r t

Start Here

q u a r t

There are four _____cup_____ s in a _____quart_____ .

TIP! You may want to offer students some extra support for these more challenging words, marked with a ★.

Name _____

Read each clue and write the answer in the blank.
Use the first and last words to fill in the sentence under the ladder.

SOCIAL STUDIES

CONNECTED COUNTRIES

7. A large land mass.
Take away the last 2 letters, then add 3.

_ _ _ _ _ _ _ _ _ _

6. To keep doing something.
Take away 3 letters.

_ _ c o u n t r _ _

5. To put an end to selling a certain product.
Add 6 letters.

_ _ _ _ _ _ _ _ _ _ _

4. A type of dance. ⭐
Take away 3 letters.

_ _ _ _ _

3. A reduced price on something.
Add 3 letters.

_ _ _ _ _ _ _ _ _

2. To list numbers in order.
Take away 1 letter.

_ _ _ _ _

1. A unit or part of a state.
Take away 1 letter.

Start Here

_ _ _ _ _ _

c o u n t r y

A _____ is a part of a _____.

TIP! You may want to offer students some extra support for these more challenging words, marked with a (★).

CONNECTED COUNTRIES
Answer Key and Teaching Notes

c o n t i n e n t

7. A large land mass.

Take away the last 2 letters, then add 3.

Have students list the seven continents on Earth (Africa, Antarctica, Asia, Australia, Europe, North America, South America).

c o n t i n u e

6. To keep doing something.

Take away 3 letters.

d i s c o n t i n u e

5. To put an end to selling a certain product.

Add 6 letters.

Have students determine the number of syllables (vowel sounds) in the word.

4. A type of dance. (★)

Take away 3 letters.

d i s c o

d i s c o u n t

3. A reduced price on something.

Add 3 letters.

2. To list numbers in order.

Take away 1 letter.

As a challenge, have students work in pairs to count backward by 7's from 100.

c o u n t

1. A unit or part of a state.

Take away 1 letter.

Start Here

c o u n t y

c o u n t r y

A ___country___ is a part of a ___continent___.

Name _____

Read each clue and write the answer in the blank.
Use the first and last words to fill in the sentence under the ladder.

SOCIAL STUDIES

YOUR VOTE COUNTS!

9. A government of the people.

Take away the last letter, then add 5.

— — — — — — — — — —

8. A kind of devil. ★

Add 1 letter, then rearrange the letters.

7. Curved roof.

Rearrange the letters.

— — — — —

6. The number that occurs most frequently in a set of numbers.

Change 2 letters.

— — — —

5. A female horse.

Add 1 letter.

— — — —

4. To damage or spoil. ★

Take away 2 letters.

— — — —

3. To walk in a military manner, often as a group.

Add 1 letter.

— — —

2. A curved doorway in architecture.

Take away 3 letters.

— — — —

★

1. An absolute single ruler of a nation.

Take away 1 letter.

Start Here

— — — — — — —

m o n a r c h y

A _____ is governed by a single ruler, while a _____ is governed by officials elected by the people.

YOUR VOTE COUNTS!
Answer Key and Teaching Notes

9. A government of the people.

Take away the last letter, then add 5.

Have students count the number of syllables (vowel sounds) in the word.

d e m o c r a c y

8. A kind of devil. ★

Add 1 letter, then rearrange the letters.

d e m o n

7. Curved roof.

Rearrange the letters.

d o m e

m o d e

6. The number that occurs most frequently in a set of numbers.

Change 2 letters.

Multiple meaning word: a way of doing something.

5. A female horse.

Add 1 letter.

m a r e

3. To walk in a military manner, often as a group.

Add 1 letter.

Multiple meaning word: as a proper noun, a month of the year.

m a r

4. To damage or spoil. ★

Take away 2 letters.

m a r c h

2. A curved doorway in architecture.

Take away 3 letters.

Multiple meaning word: combines with other words to mean *leader* or *main* (*archbishop*, *archenemy*).

a r c h

1. An absolute single ruler of a nation. ★

Take away 1 letter.

Start Here

m o n a r c h

m o n a r c h y

A _____monarchy_____ is governed by a single ruler, while a _____democracy_____ is governed by officials elected by the people.

TIP! You may want to offer students some extra support for these more challenging words, marked with a ★.

Name _____

Read each clue and write the answer in the blank.
Use the first and last words to fill in the sentence under the ladder.

SOCIAL STUDIES

REVOLUTIONARY!

11. A person who is loyal to his or her country.
Add 2 letters.

— — — — — — — —

10. A violent protest. ★
Take away 3 letters.

— — — —

9. A horse-drawn, two-wheeled vehicle.
Add 3 letters.

— — — — — — —

8. To burn. ★
Add 1 letter.

— — — —

7. A vehicle with four wheels.
Change 1 letter.

— — —

6. To damage or spoil. ★
Take away 1 letter.

— — —

5. A female horse.
Change 2 letters.

— — — —

4. A discounted item is on ____.
Change 1 letter.

— — — —

3. An Ivy League school in Connecticut.
Take away the first 2 letters, then add 1.

— — — —

2. Of kings and queens.
Change 1 letter.

— — — — —

1. Faithful.
Take away 3 letters.

Start Here

— — — — —

l o y a l i s t

During the American Revolution, people on England's side were called _____s and those who wanted to start a new country were called _____s.

REVOLUTIONARY!
Answer Key and Teaching Notes

11. A person who is loyal to his or her country.

Add 2 letters.

Have students list some patriotic holidays (Fourth of July, Memorial Day).

9. A horse-drawn, two-wheeled vehicle.

Add 3 letters.

Have students determine the number of syllables (vowel sounds) in the word.

7. A vehicle with four wheels.

Change 1 letter.

5. A female horse.

Change 2 letters.

3. An Ivy League school in Connecticut.

Take away the first 2 letters, then add 1.

1. Faithful.

Take away 3 letters.

Start Here

p a t r i o t

r i o t

c h a r i o t

c h a r

c a r

m a r

m a r e

s a l e

Y a l e

r o y a l

l o y a l

l o y a l i s t

10. A violent protest. ★

Take away 3 letters.

8. To burn. ★

Add 1 letter.

6. To damage or spoil. ★

Take away 1 letter.

4. A discounted item is on _____.

Change 1 letter.

2. Of kings and queens.

Change 1 letter.

During the American Revolution, people on England's side were called __loyalist__s and those who wanted to start a new country were called __patriot__s.

Read each clue and write the answer in the blanks.
Use the first and last words to fill in the sentence under the ladder.

SOCIAL STUDIES

FOR STARTERS

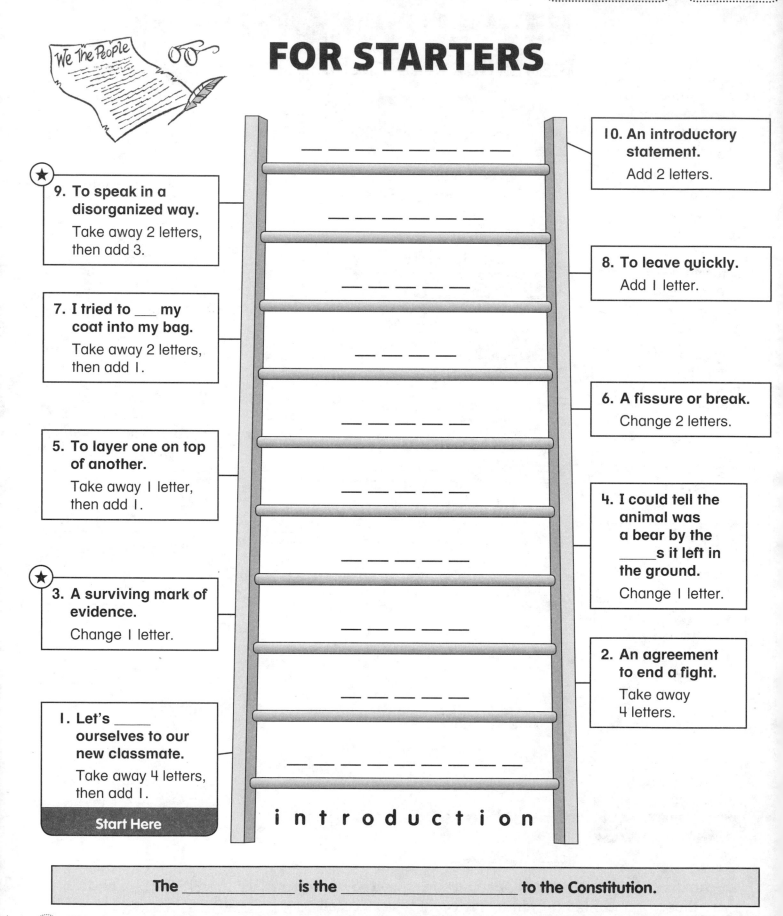

10. An introductory statement.
Add 2 letters.

★ 9. To speak in a disorganized way.
Take away 2 letters, then add 3.

8. To leave quickly.
Add 1 letter.

7. I tried to ___ my coat into my bag.
Take away 2 letters, then add 1.

6. A fissure or break.
Change 2 letters.

5. To layer one on top of another.
Take away 1 letter, then add 1.

4. I could tell the animal was a bear by the ____s it left in the ground.
Change 1 letter.

★ 3. A surviving mark of evidence.
Change 1 letter.

2. An agreement to end a fight.
Take away 4 letters.

1. Let's _____ ourselves to our new classmate.
Take away 4 letters, then add 1.

Start Here

i n t r o d u c t i o n

The _____ is the _____ to the Constitution.

FOR STARTERS
Answer Key and Teaching Notes

p r e a m b l e

r a m b l e

s c r a m

c r a m

c r a c k

s t a c k

t r a c k

t r a c e

t r u c e

i n t r o d u c e

i n t r o d u c t i o n

⭐ **9. To speak in a disorganized way.**

Take away 2 letters, then add 3.

7. I tried to ___ my coat into my bag.

Take away 2 letters, then add 1.

5. To layer one on top of another.

Take away 1 letter, then add 1.

⭐ **3. A surviving mark of evidence.**

Change 1 letter.

Multiple meaning word: to follow a trail.

1. Let's _____ ourselves to our new classmate.

Take away 4 letters, then add 1.

Start Here

10. An introductory statement.

Add 2 letters.

8. To leave quickly.

Add 1 letter.

6. A fissure or break.

Change 2 letters.

4. I could tell the animal was a bear by the _____s it left in the ground.

Change 1 letter.

2. An agreement to end a fight.

Take away 4 letters.

In pairs, have students talk about a time they called a truce with a sibling or friend.

The ___preamble___ is the ___introduction___ to the Constitution.

Read each clue and write the answer in the blanks.
Use the first and last words to fill in the sentence under the ladder.

HINT! Words with a ⭐ are more challenging!

SOCIAL STUDIES

FOLLOWING THE LAW

9. Money you pay to go to school.
Take away 2 letters.

7. Something you mean to say or do.
Add 5 letters.

5. Past tense of *lend*.
Add 1 letter.

3. An animal kept in a home as part of the family.
Change 1 letter.

1. The foot of an animal.
Take away 1 letter, then change 1.

Start Here

10. A document of principles or rules about how a country will work.
Add 5 letters (*c, o, n, s, t*), then rearrange.

8. Having a feeling about something without proof.
Change 2 letters.

6. What you sleep in when you camp.
Change 1 letter.

4. Allow.
Change 1 letter.

⭐
2. A bench with a back and arms at the end, usually in a church.
Change 1 letter.

l a w s

The _____ of the United States established America's national government and fundamental _____.

FOLLOWING THE LAW
Answer Key and Teaching Notes

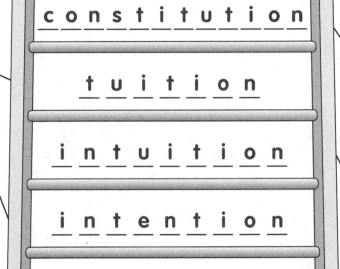

The word ladder (top to bottom):

- c o n s t i t u t i o n
- t u i t i o n
- i n t u i t i o n
- i n t e n t i o n
- t e n t
- l e n t
- l e t
- p e t
- p e w
- p a w
- l a w s

Start Here

10. A document of principles or rules about how a country will work.

Add 5 letters (*c, o, n, s, t*), then rearrange.

9. Money you pay to go to school.

Take away 2 letters.

8. Having a feeling about something without proof.

Change 2 letters.

In pairs, have students share, "A time when I had good intuition was…"

7. Something you mean to say or do.

Add 5 letters.

6. What you sleep in when you camp.

Change 1 letter.

5. Past tense of *lend*.

Add 1 letter.

Review tenses of this verb (past: *lent*; present perfect: *has lent*; present: *lend*; future: *will lend*).

4. Allow.

Change 1 letter.

3. An animal kept in a home as part of the family.

Change 1 letter.

In pairs, have students share, "My dream pet would be…"

2. A bench with a back and arms at the end, usually in a church. ★

Change 1 letter.

1. The foot of an animal.

Take away 1 letter, then change 1.

The ___Constitution___ of the United States established America's national government and fundamental ___laws___.

Name _____

Read each clue and write the answer in the blanks.
Use the first and last words to fill in the sentence under the ladder.

SOCIAL STUDIES

KNOW YOUR RIGHTS!

★ 11. A job or action that someone is accountable for.
Take away the last letter, then add 7.

`_ _ _ _ _ _ _ _ _ _`

10. A reaction.
Take away the last letter, then add 2.

`_ _ _ _ _ _ _ _ _`

★ 9. To react to something.
Add 3 letters to the beginning.

`_ _ _ _ _ _ _`

8. A small body of water.
Add 1 letter.

7. Peas grow inside of a _____.
Change 1 letter.

`_ _ _ _`

6. The frog was sitting on a lily _____.
Change 1 letter.

`_ _ _ _`

5. A skillet.
Change 1 letter.

`_ _ _ _`

4. It circulates air.
Change 1 letter.

`_ _ _ _`

3. Part of a fish that helps it swim.
Change 1 letter.

`_ _ _ _`

2. A sweet fruit.
Take away 2 letters.

`_ _ _ _`

1. An argument.
Change 1 letter.

Start Here

`r i g h t`

A _____ is a freedom that is protected, while a _____ is a duty of a citizen.

KNOW YOUR RIGHTS!
Answer Key and Teaching Notes

★ **11. A job or action that someone is accountable for.**
Take away the last letter, then add 7.
Have students count the number of syllables (vowel sounds) in the word.

★ **9. To react to something.**
Add 3 letters to the beginning.

7. Peas grow inside of a _____.
Change 1 letter.

5. A skillet.
Change 1 letter.

3. Part of a fish that helps it swim.
Change 1 letter.

1. An argument.
Change 1 letter.
Multiple meaning word: a physical altercation.

Start Here

r e s p o n s i b i l i t y
r e s p o n s e
r e s p o n d
p o n d
p o d
p a d
p a n
f a n
f i n
f i g
f i g h t
r i g h t

10. A reaction.
Take away the last letter, then add 2.

8. A small body of water.
Add 1 letter.

6. The frog was sitting on a lily _____.
Change 1 letter.

4. It circulates air.
Change 1 letter.
Multiple meaning word: Also someone who really likes someone else, often someone famous.

2. A sweet fruit.
Take away 2 letters.

A ___right___ is a freedom that is protected, while a ___responsibility___ is a duty of a citizen.

Name _____

Read each clue and write the answer in the blanks.
Use the first and last words to fill in the sentence under the ladder.

HINT! Words with a ★ are more challenging!

SOCIAL STUDIES

TO THE FLAG

11. A promise.
Add 1 letter.

_ _ _ _ _ _ _

10. The edge.
Change 1 letter.

★ **9. To live in a place for a short time.**
Add 2 letters.

_ _ _ _ _ _

8. A piece of wood.
Change 1 letter.

_ _ _ _ _ _

7. To hang back.
Change 1 letter.

_ _ _ _

6. A boy.
Take away 1 letter.

_ _ _

5. To fall to Earth.
Take away 1 letter.

_ _ _

★ **4. The pituitary ____ is in charge of hormones.**
Take away 2 letters, then add 1.

_ _ _ _

3. A quick look.
Add 1 letter.

_ _ _ _ _

★ **2. A weapon used by knights; also, to pierce.**
Take away 3 letters.

_ _ _ _ _ _

1. A group joined with common interests.
Take away 2 letters.

Start Here

_ _ _ _ _ _

_ _ _ _ _ _ _ _ _ _

a l l e g i a n c e

The _____ of _____ of the United States is an expression of loyalty and commitment to the United States.

102

TO THE FLAG
Answer Key and Teaching Notes

TIP! You may want to offer students some extra support for these more challenging words, marked with a ★.

11. A promise.
Add 1 letter.

p l e d g e

l e d g e

10. The edge.
Change 1 letter.

★ **9. To live in a place for a short time.**
Add 2 letters.
Multiple meaning word: to get caught or stuck somewhere.

l o d g e

l o g

8. A piece of wood.
Change 1 letter.

7. To hang back.
Change 1 letter.

l a g

l a d

6. A boy.
Take away 1 letter.

5. To fall to Earth.
Take away 1 letter.
Multiple meaning word: earth not covered by water.

l a n d

g l a n d

★ **4. The pituitary ____ is in charge of hormones.**
Take away 2 letters, then add 1.

3. A quick look.
Add 1 letter.
Have student list synonyms for *glance* (*glimpse, peek, look*).

g l a n c e

l a n c e

★ **2. A weapon used by knights; also, to pierce.**
Take away 3 letters.

1. A group joined with common interests.
Take away 2 letters.

Start Here

a l l i a n c e

a l l e g i a n c e

The ___Pledge___ of ___Allegiance___ of the United States is an expression of loyalty and commitment to the United States.

Read each clue and write the answer in the blanks.
Use the first and last words to fill in the sentence under the ladder.

SOCIAL STUDIES

BALANCED BRANCHES

10. The hero had super _____.
Change the first letter, then add 1.

★ 9. To crouch in fear.
Change 1 letter.

8. I had to ____ the bike with a tarp so it wouldn't get wet.
Add 1 letter.

7. A watery inlet.
Change 1 letter.

6. To collapse.
Take away 2 letters, then rearrange the remaining letters.

★ 5. To leave a place.
Take away 3 letters, then add 1.

4. A trip during a holiday.
Take away 1 letter, then add 3.

3. A country.
Change 1 letter.

★ 2. To portion out.
Take away 4 letters.

★ 1. The act of making amends.
Change 1 letter.

Start Here

s e p a r a t i o n

The _____ of _____ divides the powers of the United States government into three branches: executive, legislative, and judicial.

TIP! You may want to offer students some extra support for these more challenging words, marked with a ★.

BALANCED BRANCHES
Answer Key and Teaching Notes

9. To crouch in fear. ★
Change 1 letter.

7. A watery inlet.
Change 1 letter.

5. To leave a place. ★
Take away 3 letters, then add 1.

3. A country.
Change 1 letter.
Point out the two different pronunciations for *ration* and *nation* despite similar spellings.

1. The act of making amends. ★
Change 1 letter.
Have students count the number of syllables (vowel sounds) in the word.

Start Here

p o w e r s

c o w e r

c o v e r

c o v e

c a v e

v a c a t e

v a c a t i o n

n a t i o n

r a t i o n

r e p a r a t i o n

s e p a r a t i o n

10. The hero had super _____.
Change the first letter, then add 1.

8. I had to ____ the bike with a tarp so it wouldn't get wet.
Add 1 letter.
In pairs, have students come up with at least three different meanings for *cover*.

6. To collapse.
Take away 2 letters, then rearrange the remaining letters.

4. A trip during a holiday.
Take away 1 letter, then add 3.

2. To portion out. ★
Take away 4 letters.

The __separation__ of __powers__ divides the powers of the United States government into three branches: executive, legislative, and judicial.

Name _____

Read each clue and write the answer in the blanks.
Use the first and last words to fill in the sentence under the ladder.

HINT! Words with a ★ are more challenging!

SOCIAL STUDIES

KEEP IT IN CHECK

11. She _____ on the tightrope by keeping her arms out on either side.
Add 3 letters.

9. Moving your body to music.
Take away 1 letter, then add 2.

7. To dip underwater.
Change 1 letter.

5. To bend down.
Change 1 letter.

3. A short, quick poke, often made by a bird's beak.
Change 1 letter.

1. When I'm embarrassed, my ____ go pink.
Change 1 letter.

Start Here

— — — — — — — — — —

— — — — —

— — — — —

— — — —

— — —

— — — —

— — — —

— — — —

— — — — —

c h e c k s

10. A long wooden weapon with a sharp head or point. ★
Change 1 letter.

8. Wet and cold. ★
Change 1 letter.

6. A very large pile of sand. ★
Change 2 letters.

4. A small, round disk used to play hockey.
Change 1 letter.

2. To look at something when you know you shouldn't.
Take away 3 letters, then add 1.

In a system of _____ and _____, each branch has its own powers so that no one branch of government may become too powerful.

KEEP IT IN CHECK
Answer Key and Teaching Notes

11. She _____ on the tightrope by keeping her arms out on either side.
Add 3 letters.

9. Moving your body to music.
Take away 1 letter, then add 2.
Have students list all the types of dance they can think of (ballet, tap, jazz, hip-hop).

7. To dip underwater.
Change 1 letter.

5. To bend down.
Change 1 letter.
Multiple meaning word: a bird commonly found on lakes and ponds.

3. A short, quick poke, often made by a bird's beak.
Change 1 letter.

1. When I'm embarrassed, my __ go pink.
Change 1 letter.

Start Here

- b a l a n c e s
- l a n c e
- d a n c e
- d a n k
- d u n k
- d u n e
- d u c k
- p u c k
- p e c k
- p e e k
- c h e e k s
- c h e c k s

10. A long wooden weapon with a sharp head or point. ⭐
Change 1 letter.

8. Wet and cold. ⭐
Change 1 letter.

6. A very large pile of sand. ⭐
Change 2 letters.

4. A small, round disk used to play hockey.
Change 1 letter.
Have students name other things besides balls that are used to play sports (Frisbee, javelin, discus, skateboard).

2. To look at something when you know you shouldn't.
Take away 3 letters, then add 1.

In a system of ___**checks**___ and ___**balances**___, each branch has its own powers so that no one branch of government may become too powerful.

Read each clue and write the answer in the blanks.
Use the first and last words to fill in the sentence under the ladder.

HINT! Words with a ★ are more challenging!

SOCIAL STUDIES

HEAD OF STATE

11. Head of the executive branch of government.
Add 1 letter.

— — — — — — — — —

10. A person who lives in a place.
Add 2 letters.

— — — — — — — — —

★ 9. To live in a place.
Add 2 letters.

— — — — — — —

8. I went for a ____ on my new motorcycle.
Change 1 letter.

— — — — —

★ 7. A ritual.
Change 1 letter.

— — — — —

6. To score or judge.
Take away 2 letters.

— — — — —

5. To connect one thing to another.
Add 2 letters.

— — — — — — —

4. Arriving after the appointed time to an event.
Change 1 letter.

— — — — —

★ 3. A type of string instrument.
Change 1 letter.

— — — — —

2. Adorable, attractive.
Take away 3 letters.

1. To carry out an order.
Take away 2 letters.

— — — — — — —

Start Here

e x e c u t i v e

The _____ branch is made up of the cabinet and the _____ of the United States.

HEAD OF STATE
Answer Key and Teaching Notes

11. Head of the executive branch of government.
Add 1 letter.

p r e s i d e n t

10. A person who lives in a place.
Add 2 letters.
Have students count the number of syllables (vowel sounds) in the word.

r e s i d e n t

★ **9. To live in a place.**
Add 2 letters.

r e s i d e

r i d e

8. I went for a _____ on my new motorcycle.
Change 1 letter.

★ **7. A ritual.**
Change 1 letter.
Homophone: *right*, correct, or opposite of *left*.

r i t e

r a t e

6. To score or judge.
Take away 2 letters.

5. To connect one thing to another.
Add 2 letters.

r e l a t e

l a t e

4. Arriving after the appointed time to an event.
Change 1 letter.

★ **3. A type of string instrument.**
Change 1 letter.
Show students a digital image of a lute.

l u t e

2. Adorable, attractive.
Take away 3 letters.

c u t e

1. To carry out an order.
Take away 2 letters.

Start Here

e x e c u t e

e x e c u t i v e

The ___executive___ branch is made up of the cabinet and the ___President___ of the United States.

Name _____

Read each clue and write the answer in the blanks.
Use the first and last words to fill in the sentence under the ladder.

SOCIAL STUDIES

IN THE WHITE HOUSE

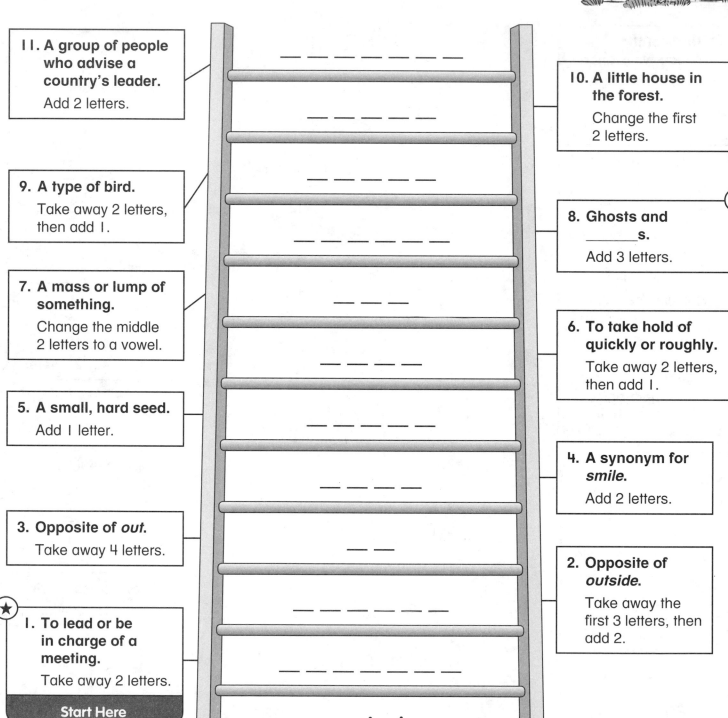

11. A group of people who advise a country's leader.
Add 2 letters.

9. A type of bird.
Take away 2 letters, then add 1.

7. A mass or lump of something.
Change the middle 2 letters to a vowel.

5. A small, hard seed.
Add 1 letter.

3. Opposite of *out*.
Take away 4 letters.

⭐ 1. To lead or be in charge of a meeting.
Take away 2 letters.

Start Here

10. A little house in the forest.
Change the first 2 letters.

⭐ 8. Ghosts and _____s.
Add 3 letters.

6. To take hold of quickly or roughly.
Take away 2 letters, then add 1.

4. A synonym for *smile*.
Add 2 letters.

2. Opposite of *outside*.
Take away the first 3 letters, then add 2.

p r e s i d e n t

The _____ is made up of the vice president and advisors appointed by the _____.

110

IN THE WHITE HOUSE
Answer Key and Teaching Notes

11. A group of people who advise a country's leader.
Add 2 letters.

c a b i n e t

10. A little house in the forest.
Change the first 2 letters.

c a b i n

9. A type of bird.
Take away 2 letters, then add 1.

r o b i n

8. Ghosts and _____s. ★
Add 3 letters.

g o b l i n

7. A mass or lump of something.
Change the middle 2 letters to a vowel.
Have students list synonyms of gob (a lot, many, a ton).

g o b

6. To take hold of quickly or roughly.
Take away 2 letters, then add 1.

g r a b

5. A small, hard seed.
Add 1 letter.
Have students name things whose units are grains (sand, salt, wheat).

g r a i n

4. A synonym for smile.
Add 2 letters.

g r i n

3. Opposite of out.
Take away 4 letters.

i n

2. Opposite of outside.
Take away the first 3 letters, then add 2.

i n s i d e

★ **1. To lead or be in charge of a meeting.**
Take away 2 letters.

Start Here

p r e s i d e

p r e s i d e n t

The ___cabinet___ is made up of the vice president and advisors appointed by the ___president___ .

Name _____

Read each clue and write the answer in the blanks.
Use the first and last words to fill in the sentence under the ladder.

HINT! Words with a ⭐ are more challenging!

SOCIAL STUDIES

MAKING THE RULES

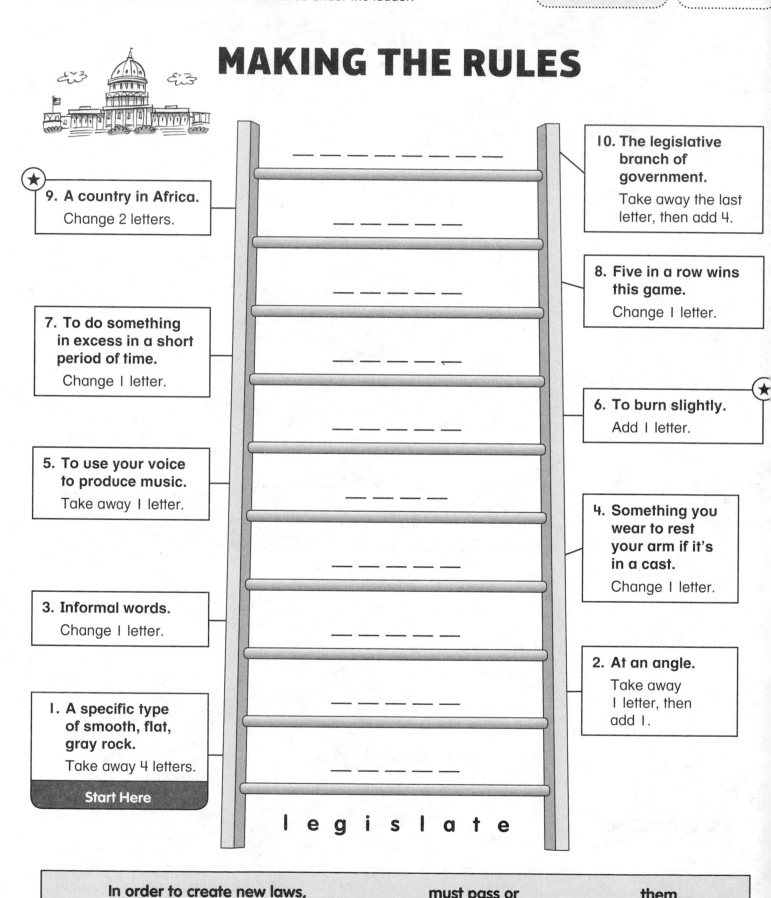

⭐ **9. A country in Africa.**
Change 2 letters.

7. To do something in excess in a short period of time.
Change 1 letter.

5. To use your voice to produce music.
Take away 1 letter.

3. Informal words.
Change 1 letter.

1. A specific type of smooth, flat, gray rock.
Take away 4 letters.

Start Here

10. The legislative branch of government.
Take away the last letter, then add 4.

8. Five in a row wins this game.
Change 1 letter.

6. To burn slightly. ⭐
Add 1 letter.

4. Something you wear to rest your arm if it's in a cast.
Change 1 letter.

2. At an angle.
Take away 1 letter, then add 1.

l e g i s l a t e

In order to create new laws, _____ must pass or _____ them.

MAKING THE RULES
Answer Key and Teaching Notes

Congress

10. The legislative branch of government.
Take away the last letter, then add 4.

★ 9. A country in Africa.
Change 2 letters.

Congo

Bingo

7. To do something in excess in a short period of time.
Change 1 letter.

8. Five in a row wins this game.
Change 1 letter.
Multiple meaning word: a response when someone has the right answer.

binge

5. To use your voice to produce music.
Take away 1 letter.
In pairs, have students repeat and complete the sentence, "I like to sing when…"

singe

sing

★ 6. To burn slightly.
Add 1 letter.

3. Informal words.
Change 1 letter.
Have students list common slang words (*buck* for "dollar", *chill* for "relax").

sling

slang

4. Something you wear to rest your arm if it's in a cast.
Change 1 letter.

slant

2. At an angle.
Take away 1 letter, then add 1.

1. A specific type of smooth, flat, gray rock.
Take away 4 letters.

Start Here

slate

legislate

In order to create new laws, ___Congress___ must pass or ___legislate___ them.

Name _____

Read each clue and write the answer in the blanks.
Use the first and last words to fill in the sentence under the ladder.

SOCIAL STUDIES

CHANGE THE WORLD

★ **11. To change to make better or more accurate.**
Add 1 letter.

10. A word showing agreement, often after a prayer.
Add 1 letter.

9. Not women, but ____.
Take away 1 letter.

8. Unkind.
Change 1 letter.

7. To rest against something.
Change 1 letter.

6. To jump high in the air.
Change 1 letter.

5. To pile up.
Take away 1 letter.

4. Inexpensive.
Change 2 letters.

3. To chant encouragement.
Take away 1 letter, then add 2.

2. To burn.
Take away 2 letters.

1. A fee.
Change 1 letter.

Start Here

c h a n g e

To _____ a law means to _____ it.

CHANGE THE WORLD
Answer Key and Teaching Notes

★

11. To change to make better or more accurate.
Add 1 letter.

a m e n d

10. A word showing agreement, often after a prayer.
Add 1 letter.

a m e n

9. Not women, but ____.
Take away 1 letter.

m e n

8. Unkind.
Change 1 letter.
Multiple meaning word: the average of something.

m e a n

7. To rest against something.
Change 1 letter.
Multiple meaning word: *skinny*.

l e a n

6. To jump high in the air.
Change 1 letter.
Have students list synonyms for *leap* (*jump*, *bound*, *hop*, *spring*).

l e a p

5. To pile up.
Take away 1 letter.

h e a p

4. Inexpensive.
Change 2 letters.

c h e a p

3. To chant encouragement.
Take away 1 letter, then add 2.

c h e e r

2. To burn.
Take away 2 letters.

c h a r

1. A fee.
Change 1 letter.

c h a r g e

Start Here

c h a n g e

To _____amend_____ a law means to _____change_____ it.

Name _____

Read each clue and write the answer in the blanks.
Use the first and last words to fill in the sentence under the ladder.

HINT! Words with a ★ are more challenging!

SOCIAL STUDIES

ORDER!

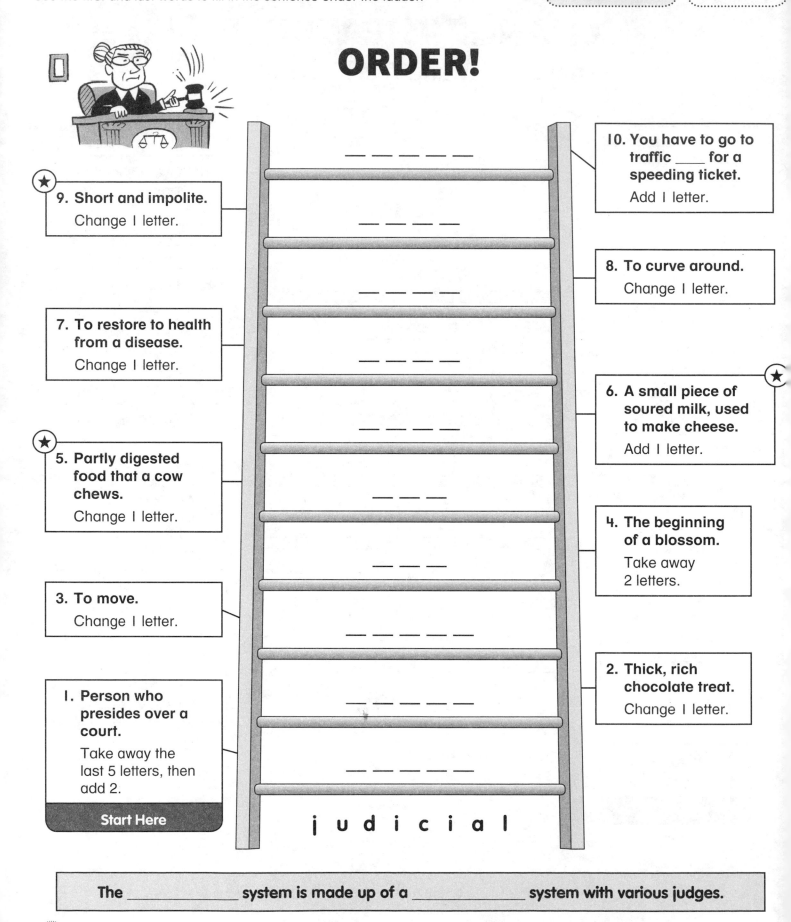

10. You have to go to traffic ____ for a speeding ticket.
Add 1 letter.

★ 9. Short and impolite.
Change 1 letter.

8. To curve around.
Change 1 letter.

7. To restore to health from a disease.
Change 1 letter.

★ 6. A small piece of soured milk, used to make cheese.
Add 1 letter.

★ 5. Partly digested food that a cow chews.
Change 1 letter.

4. The beginning of a blossom.
Take away 2 letters.

3. To move.
Change 1 letter.

2. Thick, rich chocolate treat.
Change 1 letter.

1. Person who presides over a court.
Take away the last 5 letters, then add 2.

Start Here

_ _ _ _ _ _

_ _ _ _ _

_ _ _ _

_ _ _ _ _

_ _ _ _

_ _ _

_ _ _

_ _ _ _ _

_ _ _ _ _

_ _ _ _ _

j u d i c i a l

The _____ system is made up of a _____ system with various judges.

ORDER!
Answer Key and Teaching Notes

10. You have to go to traffic _____ for a speeding ticket.
Add 1 letter.

9. Short and impolite.
Change 1 letter.
In pairs, have students share, "When someone talks to me in a curt way, it makes me feel…"

8. To curve around.
Change 1 letter.
Multiple meaning word: a lock of hair that twists in a spiral.

7. To restore to health from a disease.
Change 1 letter.

★ **6. A small piece of soured milk, used to make cheese.**
Add 1 letter.

★ **5. Partly digested food that a cow chews.**
Change 1 letter.

4. The beginning of a blossom.
Take away 2 letters.

3. To move.
Change 1 letter.

2. Thick, rich chocolate treat.
Change 1 letter.
Multiple meaning word: to cheat or make something up.

1. Person who presides over a court.
Take away the last 5 letters, then add 2.

Start Here

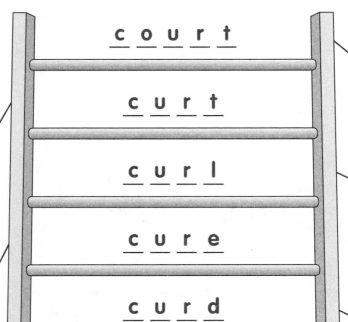

court
curt
curl
cure
curd
cud
bud
budge
fudge
judge
judicial

The __judicial__ system is made up of a __court__ system with various judges.

Read each clue and write the answer in the blanks.
Use the first and last words to fill in the sentence under the ladder.

HINT! Words with a ★ are more challenging!

SOCIAL STUDIES

LOCAL & NATIONAL

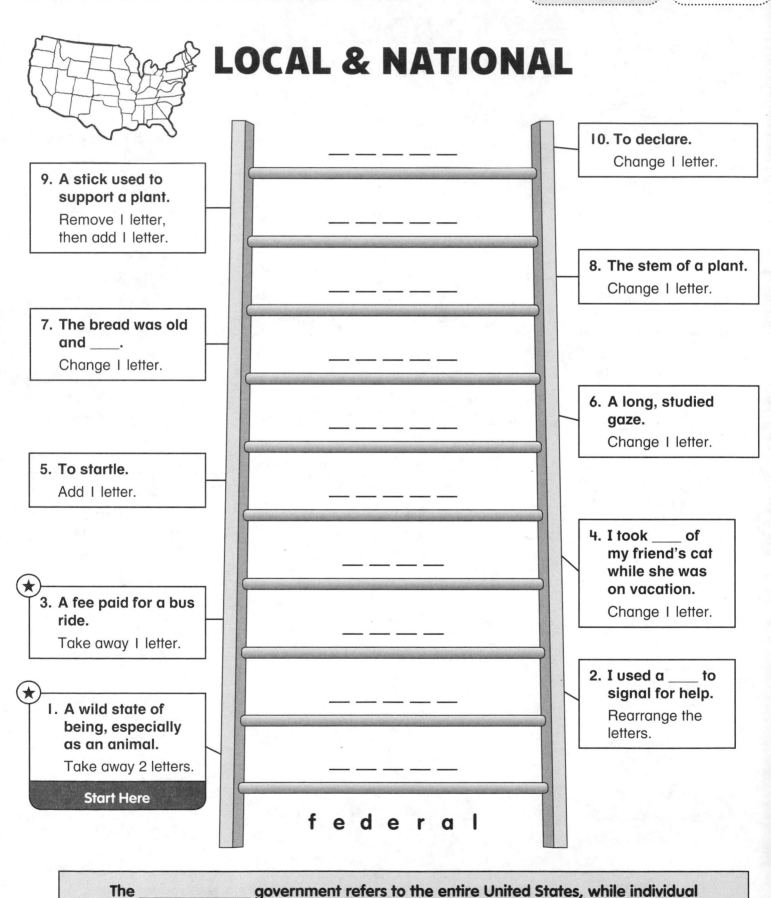

10. To declare.
Change 1 letter.
_ _ _ _ _

9. A stick used to support a plant.
Remove 1 letter, then add 1 letter.
_ _ _ _ _

8. The stem of a plant.
Change 1 letter.
_ _ _ _ _

7. The bread was old and ____.
Change 1 letter.
_ _ _ _ _

6. A long, studied gaze.
Change 1 letter.
_ _ _ _ _

5. To startle.
Add 1 letter.
_ _ _ _ _

4. I took ____ of my friend's cat while she was on vacation.
Change 1 letter.
_ _ _ _

★ 3. A fee paid for a bus ride.
Take away 1 letter.
_ _ _ _

★ 1. A wild state of being, especially as an animal.
Take away 2 letters.

2. I used a ____ to signal for help.
Rearrange the letters.
_ _ _ _ _

Start Here

f e d e r a l

The _____ government refers to the entire United States, while individual _____s each have their own governments.

LOCAL & NATIONAL
Answer Key and Teaching Notes

s t a t e

10. To declare.
Change 1 letter.

9. A stick used to support a plant.
Remove 1 letter, then add 1 letter.
Homophone: *steak*, a cut of meat.

s t a k e

8. The stem of a plant.
Change 1 letter.

s t a l k

7. The bread was old and ____.
Change 1 letter.

s t a l e

6. A long, studied gaze.
Change 1 letter.
Homophone: *stair*, something used to go up and down flights of a building.

5. To startle.
Add 1 letter.

s t a r e

s c a r e

⭐ **3. A fee paid for a bus ride.**
Take away 1 letter.
Homophone: *fair*, something that is honest or evenly given.

c a r e

4. I took ____ of my friend's cat while she was on vacation.
Change 1 letter.

f a r e

2. I used a ____ to signal for help.
Rearrange the letters.

f l a r e

⭐ **1. A wild state of being, especially as an animal.**
Take away 2 letters.

Start Here

f e r a l

f e d e r a l

The ___federal___ government refers to the entire United States, while individual ___state___s each have their own governments.

Read each clue and write the answer in the blanks.
Use the first and last words to fill in the sentence under the ladder.

SOCIAL STUDIES

LOCAL LEADERS

11. The leader of a city.
Add 2 letters.
— — — — —

10. A word used to express possibility.
Change 1 letter.
— — —

9. Another word for *angry*.
Take away the first 2 letters, then add 1.
— — —

8. Opposite of *follow*.
Rearrange the letters.
— — — — —

7. A business transaction.
Change 1 letter.
— — — —

★ **6. The head of a university department.**
Add 1 letter.
— — — —

★ **5. A lair or shelter for a wild animal.**
Change 1 letter.
— — —

4. 6 + 4 = __
Take away 2 letters.
— — —

3. Occurring frequently.
Take away 1 letter, then add 2.
— — — — —

2. What you use to bake something.
Change 1 letter.
— — — —

1. Opposite of *under*.
Take away 4 letters.

Start Here
— — — —

g o v e r n o r

The _____ is the head of a state, while the _____ is the head of a city.

TIP! You may want to offer students some extra support for these more challenging words, marked with a ★.

LOCAL LEADERS

Answer Key and Teaching Notes

11. The leader of a city.
Add 2 letters.

m a y o r

10. A word used to express possibility.
Change 1 letter.

m a y

9. Another word for *angry*.
Take away the first 2 letters, then add 1.

m a d

8. Opposite of *follow*.
Rearrange the letters.
Homograph: (noun) what is inside a pencil.

l e a d

7. A business transaction.
Change 1 letter.
Multiple meaning word: to manage something.

d e a l

★ **6. The head of a university department.**
Add 1 letter.

d e a n

★ **5. A lair or shelter for a wild animal.**
Change 1 letter.

d e n

4. 6 + 4 = __
Take away 2 letters.

t e n

3. Occurring frequently.
Take away 1 letter, then add 2.

o f t e n

2. What you use to bake something.
Change 1 letter.

o v e n

1. Opposite of *under*.
Take away 4 letters.
Figure of speech: *I'm over it*—when you've moved beyond something, it doesn't bother you anymore.

o v e r

Start Here

g o v e r n o r

The governor is the head of a state, while the mayor is the head of a city.

Read each clue and write the answer in the blanks.
Use the first and last words to fill in the sentence under the ladder.

WORK IT OUT

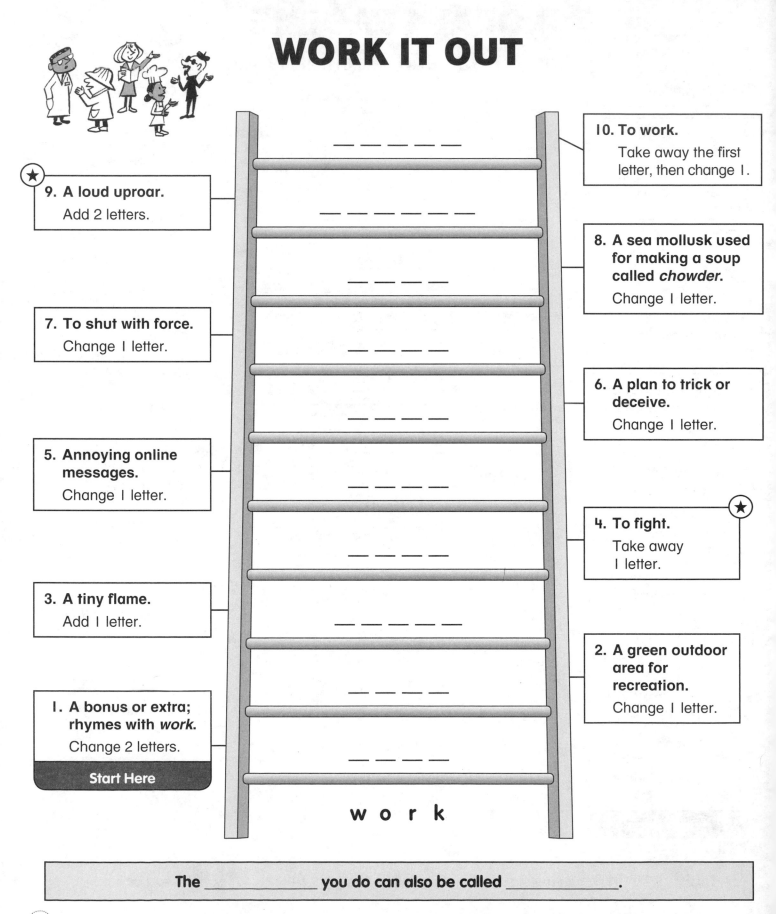

10. To work.
Take away the first letter, then change 1.

⭐ 9. A loud uproar.
Add 2 letters.

8. A sea mollusk used for making a soup called *chowder*.
Change 1 letter.

7. To shut with force.
Change 1 letter.

6. A plan to trick or deceive.
Change 1 letter.

5. Annoying online messages.
Change 1 letter.

⭐ 4. To fight.
Take away 1 letter.

3. A tiny flame.
Add 1 letter.

2. A green outdoor area for recreation.
Change 1 letter.

1. A bonus or extra; rhymes with *work*.
Change 2 letters.

Start Here

w o r k

The _____ you do can also be called _____.

TIP! You may want to offer students some extra support for these more challenging words, marked with a ★.

WORK IT OUT

Answer Key and Teaching Notes

l a b o r

c l a m o r

c l a m

s l a m

s c a m

s p a m

s p a r

s p a r k

p a r k

p e r k

w o r k

10. To work.
Take away the first letter, then change 1.
Have students list other words that contain the root *labor* (*laboratory, collaborate, elaborate, laborer*).

★ **9. A loud uproar.**
Add 2 letters.

8. A sea mollusk used for making a soup called *chowder*.
Change 1 letter.

7. To shut with force.
Change 1 letter.

6. A plan to trick or deceive.
Change 1 letter.

5. Annoying online messages.
Change 1 letter.
Discuss with students what to do when they receive spam (delete for safety).

★ **4. To fight.**
Take away 1 letter.

3. A tiny flame.
Add 1 letter.
Multiple meaning word: to stimulate interest or an idea.

2. A green outdoor area for recreation.
Change 1 letter.

1. A bonus or extra; rhymes with *work*.
Change 2 letters.

Start Here

The work **you do can also be called** labor**.**

Name _____

Read each clue and write the answer in the blanks.
Use the first and last words to fill in the sentence under the ladder.

SOCIAL STUDIES

WORKING HARD

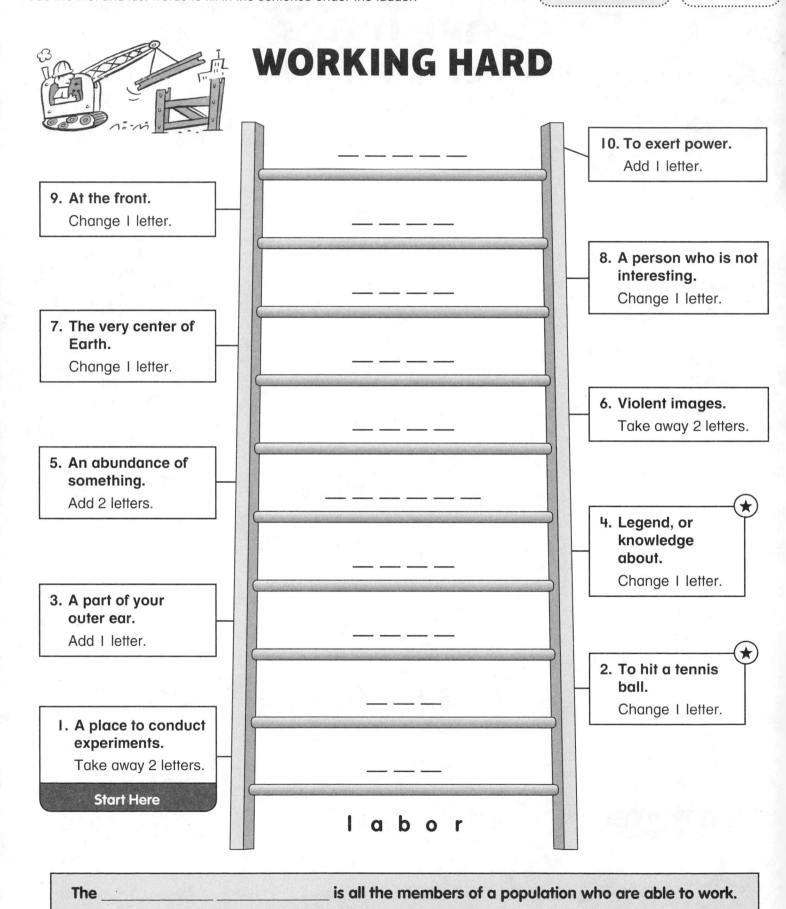

10. **To exert power.**
Add 1 letter.

9. **At the front.**
Change 1 letter.

8. **A person who is not interesting.**
Change 1 letter.

7. **The very center of Earth.**
Change 1 letter.

6. **Violent images.**
Take away 2 letters.

5. **An abundance of something.**
Add 2 letters.

4. ★ **Legend, or knowledge about.**
Change 1 letter.

3. **A part of your outer ear.**
Add 1 letter.

2. ★ **To hit a tennis ball.**
Change 1 letter.

1. **A place to conduct experiments.**
Take away 2 letters.

Start Here

l a b o r

The _____ _____ is all the members of a population who are able to work.

TIP! You may want to offer students some extra support for these more challenging words, marked with a ⭐.

WORKING HARD
Answer Key and Teaching Notes

10. To exert power.
Add 1 letter.

f o r c e

9. At the front.
Change 1 letter.

f o r e

8. A person who is not interesting.
Change 1 letter.

b o r e

7. The very center of Earth.
Change 1 letter.
Have students list other things that can be said to have a core (body, apple, sun).

c o r e

6. Violent images.
Take away 2 letters.

g o r e

5. An abundance of something.
Add 2 letters.

g a l o r e

⭐ **4. Legend, or knowledge about.**
Change 1 letter.
In pairs, have students share something they are skilled in the lore of.

l o r e

3. A part of your outer ear.
Add 1 letter.
Show students which part of the ear is the lobe.

l o b e

⭐ **2. To hit a tennis ball.**
Change 1 letter.

l o b

1. A place to conduct experiments.
Take away 2 letters.

Start Here

l a b

l a b o r

The ___labor___ ___force___ is all the members of a population who are able to work.

Read each clue and write the answer in the blanks.
Use the first and last words to fill in the sentence under the ladder.

HINT! Words with a ★ are more challenging!

SOCIAL STUDIES

MAKING MONEY

11. Money.
Take away 1 letter, then add 2.

_ _ _ _ _ _ _ _

9. Monthly payment for a living space.
Change 1 letter.

_ _ _ _ _ _ _

10. The ____ in the river was moving quickly.
Add 3 letters.

_ _ _ _

★ **7. To joke or tease.**
Take away the first 2 letters, then add 1.

_ _ _ _

8. The burglar ____ a pin to pick the lock.
Change the first and third letters.

_ _ _ _

5. ____ the number of beans in the jar.
Take away 1 letter, then add 2.

_ _ _ _ _ _

6. A visitor in someone's home.
Change 1 letter.

_ _ _ _ _

★ **3. A young woman.**
Change 1 letter.

_ _ _ _

4. Opposite of *more*.
Change 1 letter.

_ _ _ _

1. The group of actors in a play or movie.
Change 1 letter.

Start Here

_ _ _ _

2. If you're at the end of a line, you are ____.
Change 1 letter.

c a s h

The _____ is the money system used in a country, while _____ is the actual money in the form of coins and bills.

TIP! You may want to offer students some extra support for these more challenging words, marked with a ★.

MAKING MONEY
Answer Key and Teaching Notes

11. Money.
Take away 1 letter, then add 2.

c u r r e n c y

9. Monthly payment for a living space.
Change 1 letter.

c u r r e n t

7. To joke or tease.
Take away the first 2 letters, then add 1.

r e n t

5. _____ the number of beans in the jar.
Take away 1 letter, then add 2.

b e n t

★

3. A young woman.
Change 1 letter.

j e s t

1. The group of actors in a play or movie.
Change 1 letter.
Multiple meaning word: something you wear on your body to protect an injured body part.

g u e s t

Start Here

g u e s s

l e s s

l a s s

l a s t

c a s t

c a s h

10. The ____ in the river was moving quickly.
Add 3 letters.
If students are unfamiliar with this word, share a video of a running river to show the current.

8. The burglar ____ a pin to pick the lock.
Change the first and third letters.

6. A visitor in someone's home.
Change 1 letter.

4. Opposite of *more*.
Change 1 letter.

2. If you're at the end of a line, you are __.
Change 1 letter.

The ___currency___ is the money system used in a country, while ___cash___ is the actual money in the form of coins and bills.

Name _____

Read each clue and write the answer in the blanks.
Use the first and last words to fill in the sentence under the ladder.

HINT! Words with a ★ are more challenging!

SOCIAL STUDIES

RISKS & REWARDS

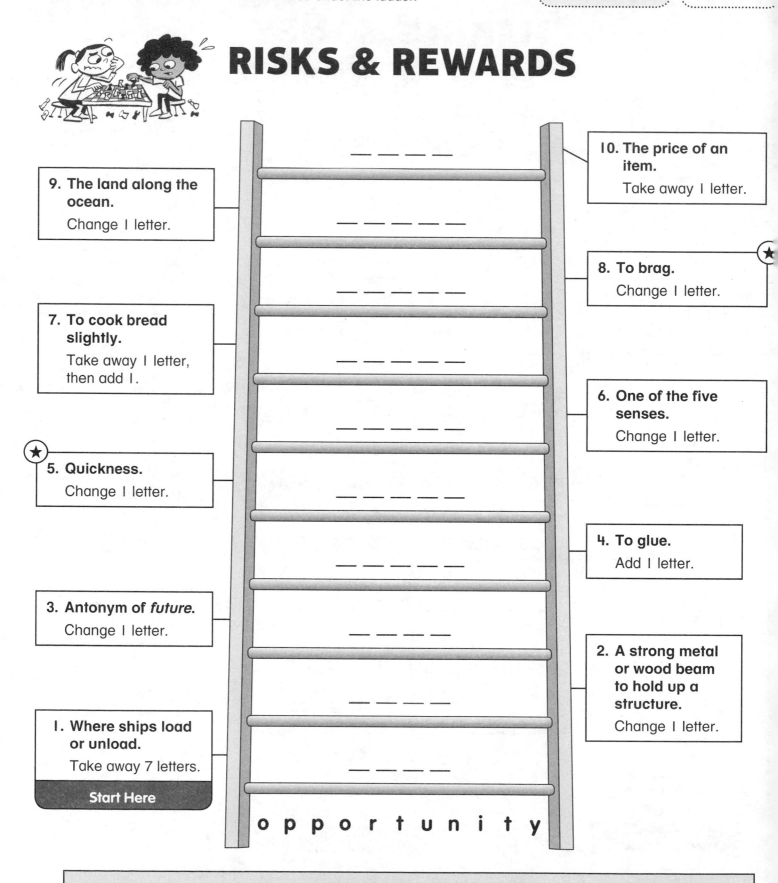

10. **The price of an item.**
Take away 1 letter.

9. **The land along the ocean.**
Change 1 letter.

8. **To brag.**
Change 1 letter. ★

7. **To cook bread slightly.**
Take away 1 letter, then add 1.

6. **One of the five senses.**
Change 1 letter.

★ 5. **Quickness.**
Change 1 letter.

4. **To glue.**
Add 1 letter.

3. **Antonym of** *future*.
Change 1 letter.

2. **A strong metal or wood beam to hold up a structure.**
Change 1 letter.

1. **Where ships load or unload.**
Take away 7 letters.

Start Here

o p p o r t u n i t y

_____ _____ is the loss of potential gain from other alternatives when one alternative is chosen.

RISKS & REWARDS
Answer Key and Teaching Notes

c o s t

c o a s t

b o a s t

t o a s t

t a s t e

h a s t e

p a s t e

p a s t

p o s t

p o r t

o p p o r t u n i t y

Start Here

9. The land along the ocean.
Change 1 letter.

7. To cook bread slightly.
Take away 1 letter, then add 1.
Multiple meaning word: a speech given at a ceremony.

⭐ **5. Quickness.**
Change 1 letter.

3. Antonym of *future*.
Change 1 letter.
Homophone: *passed*, getting a satisfactory grade on a test.

1. Where ships load or unload.
Take away 7 letters.

10. The price of an item.
Take away 1 letter.

⭐ **8. To brag.**
Change 1 letter.

6. One of the five senses.
Change 1 letter.
Have students list the other four senses (*sight, smell, touch, hearing*).

4. To glue.
Add 1 letter.

2. A strong metal or wood beam to hold up a structure.
Change 1 letter.
Multiple meaning word: to publish text or photos on social media.

_____Opportunity_____ ____cost____ is the loss of potential gain from other alternatives when one alternative is chosen.

Name _____

Read each clue and write the answer in the blanks.
Use the first and last words to fill in the sentence under the ladder.

HINT! Words with a (★) are more challenging!

SOCIAL STUDIES

THAT'S MY BUSINESS

11. A place for the sale of goods.
Add 2 letters.

_ _ _ _ _ _ _

10. A visible sign or cut that is made on something.
Change 1 letter.

_ _ _ _ _

9. Sound made by a dog.
Change 1 letter, then rearrange the letters.

_ _ _ _

8. To cook in an oven.
Take away 1 letter, then rearrange the remaining letters.

_ _ _ _

(★) **7. Describes bare or desolate places.**
Add 1 letter.

_ _ _ _ _ _

6. What happens if a water pipe cracks.
Change 1 letter.

_ _ _ _

5. The bill or mouthpart of a bird.
Change 1 letter.

_ _ _ _

(★) **4. A long piece of metal, wood, or light.**
Change 1 letter.

_ _ _ _

3. A group of people who work together, often in sports.
Add 1 letter.

_ _ _

2. A drink that can be served hot or cold.
Change 1 letter.

1. What props up a golf ball so it can be hit.
Take away 2 letters, then add 1.

_ _ _

Start Here

f r e e

The _____ _____ is an economic system in which prices are determined by private businesses and competition.

130

THAT'S MY BUSINESS
Answer Key and Teaching Notes

11. A place for the sale of goods.
Add 2 letters.

9. Sound made by a dog.
Change 1 letter, then rearrange the letters.

⭐ **7. Describes bare or desolate places.**
Add 1 letter.
Figure of speech: if a situation *looks bleak,* it means the outcome looks bad.

5. The bill or mouthpart of a bird.
Change 1 letter.

3. A group of people who work together, often in sports.
Add 1 letter.

1. What props up a golf ball so it can be hit.
Take away 2 letters, then add 1.

Start Here

m a r k e t

m a r k

b a r k

b a k e

b l e a k

l e a k

b e a k

b e a m

t e a m

t e a

t e e

f r e e

10. A visible sign or cut that is made on something.
Change 1 letter.
Figure of speech: *on your mark,* a command to get in place to begin a race.

8. To cook in an oven.
Take away 1 letter, then rearrange the remaining letters.

6. What happens if a water pipe cracks.
Change 1 letter.

⭐ **4. A long piece of metal, wood, or light.**
Change 1 letter.

2. A drink that can be served hot or cold.
Change 1 letter.
Homophone: *tee,* slang for a T-shirt.

The ___**free**___ ___**market**___ is an economic system in which prices are determined by private businesses and competition.

Read each clue and write the answer in the blanks.
Use the first and last words to fill in the sentence under the ladder.

HINT! Words with a ★ are more challenging!

SOCIAL STUDIES

WHILE SUPPLIES LAST

10. **To ask with authority.**
Change 3 letters.

★ 9. **To move someone down a level.**
Add 1 letter.

★ 8. **To show emotion.**
Take away 1 letter.

7. **You can change channels using the _____ control.**
Change 2 letters.

6. **To create again.**
Add 2 letters.

5. **To create.**
Take away 2 letters.

4. **A place where people can buy and sell goods.**
Take away 5 letters.

3. **A large grocery store.**
Add 6 letters.

2. **A synonym for** *wonderful*.
Take away 1 letter.

1. **Another word for** *dinner*.
Change 2 letters.

Start Here

s u p p l y

_____ is how much of a product or service is available, while _____
refers to the desire of buyers for the product or service.

> TIP! You may want to offer students some extra support for these more challenging words, marked with a ⭐.

WHILE SUPPLIES LAST
Answer Key and Teaching Notes

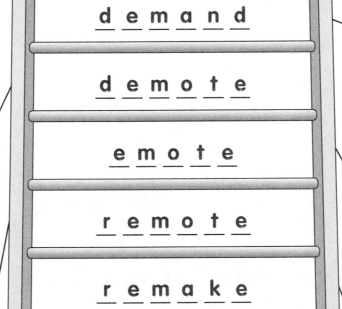

⭐

9. To move someone down a level.

Add 1 letter.

Have students list reasons someone might get demoted in his or her job (not coming to work on time, not following rules, not doing the job well).

7. You can change channels using the _____ control.

Change 2 letters.

5. To create.

Take away 2 letters.

3. A large grocery store.

Add 6 letters.

1. Another word for dinner.

Change 2 letters.

Start Here

d e m a n d

d e m o t e

e m o t e

r e m o t e

r e m a k e

m a k e

m a r k e t

s u p e r m a r k e t

s u p e r

s u p p e r

s u p p l y

10. To ask with authority.

Change 3 letters.

⭐

8. To show emotion.

Take away 1 letter.

Note that the root *mote* means "to move." What do *remote*, *emote*, *motor*, *motel*, and *motion* have to do with moving?

6. To create again.

Add 2 letters.

4. A place where people can buy and sell goods.

Take away 5 letters.

2. A synonym for *wonderful*.

Take away 1 letter.

Have students list synonyms of *super* (*magnificent*, *outstanding*, *fantastic*).

_____Supply_____ is how much of a product or service is available, while ____demand____ refers to the desire of buyers for the product or service.

Read each clue and write the answer in the blanks.
Use the first and last words to fill in the sentence under the ladder.

SOCIAL STUDIES

ALL NATURAL

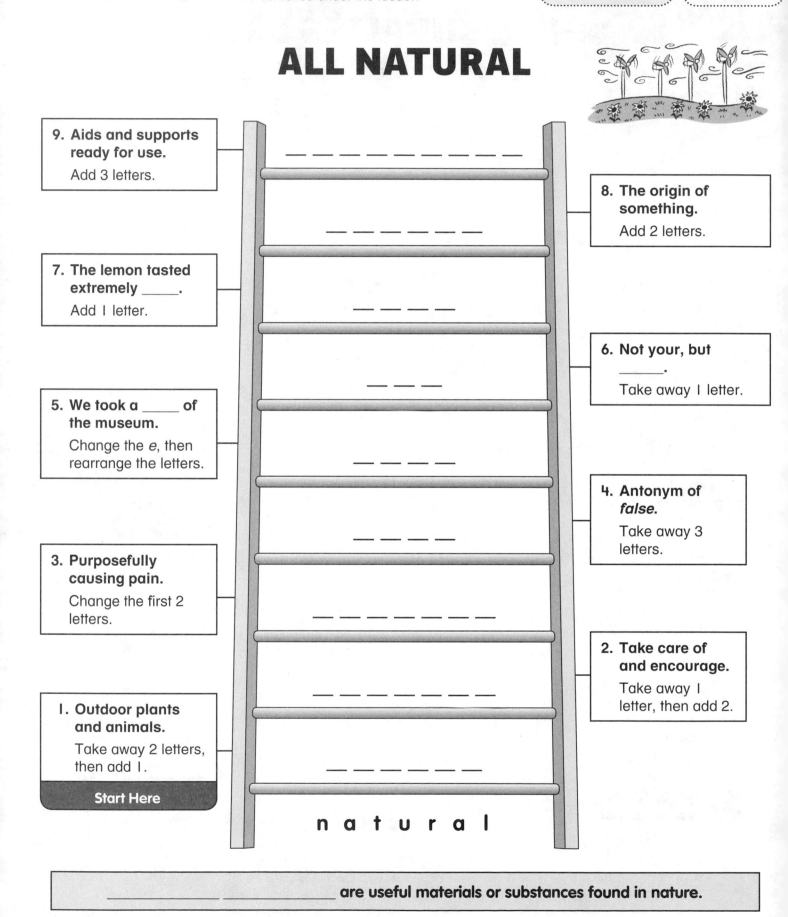

9. Aids and supports ready for use.

Add 3 letters.

— — — — — — — — — —

8. The origin of something.

Add 2 letters.

7. The lemon tasted extremely _____.

Add 1 letter.

6. Not your, but _____.

Take away 1 letter.

5. We took a _____ of the museum.

Change the *e*, then rearrange the letters.

4. Antonym of *false*.

Take away 3 letters.

3. Purposefully causing pain.

Change the first 2 letters.

2. Take care of and encourage.

Take away 1 letter, then add 2.

1. Outdoor plants and animals.

Take away 2 letters, then add 1.

Start Here

n a t u r a l

_____ _____ are useful materials or substances found in nature.

TIP! You may want to offer students some extra support for these more challenging words, marked with a ★.

ALL NATURAL
Answer Key and Teaching Notes

9. Aids and supports ready for use.
Add 3 letters.

r e s o u r c e s

8. The origin of something.
Add 2 letters.

s o u r c e

7. The lemon tasted extremely _____.
Add 1 letter.
In pairs, have students share, "I do/do not like sour candy because…"

s o u r

6. Not your, but _____.
Take away 1 letter.
Homophone: *hour*, a length of time, 60 minutes.

o u r

5. We took a _____ of the museum.
Change the *e*, then rearrange the letters.

t o u r

3. Purposefully causing pain.
Change the first 2 letters.
Have students count the number of syllables (vowel sounds) in the word.

t r u e

4. Antonym of *false*.
Take away 3 letters.

t o r t u r e

2. Take care of and encourage.
Take away 1 letter, then add 2.

n u r t u r e

1. Outdoor plants and animals.
Take away 2 letters, then add 1.

Start Here

n a t u r e

n a t u r a l

_____Natural_____ _____resources_____ are useful materials or substances found in nature.

Read each clue and write the answer in the blanks.
Use the first and last words to fill in the sentence under the ladder.

SOCIAL STUDIES

CITYSIDE, COUNTRYSIDE

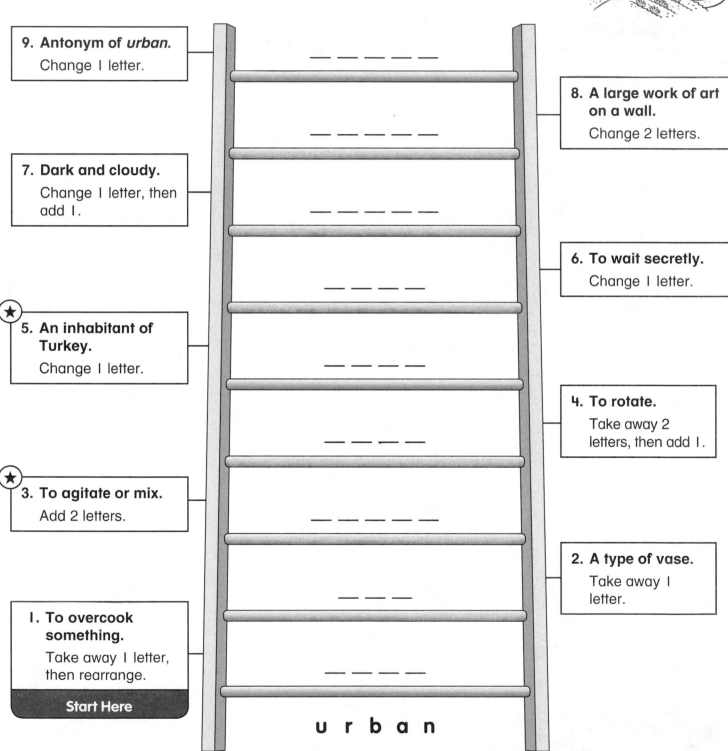

9. Antonym of *urban*.
Change 1 letter.

_ _ _ _ _

8. A large work of art on a wall.
Change 2 letters.

_ _ _ _ _

7. Dark and cloudy.
Change 1 letter, then add 1.

_ _ _ _ _

6. To wait secretly.
Change 1 letter.

_ _ _ _

★ **5. An inhabitant of Turkey.**
Change 1 letter.

_ _ _ _

4. To rotate.
Take away 2 letters, then add 1.

_ _ _ _

★ **3. To agitate or mix.**
Add 2 letters.

_ _ _ _ _

2. A type of vase.
Take away 1 letter.

_ _ _

1. To overcook something.
Take away 1 letter, then rearrange.

_ _ _ _

Start Here

u r b a n

_____ areas are more densely populated than _____ areas and can include towns and cities.

TIP! You may want to offer students some extra support for these more challenging words, marked with a ⭐.

CITYSIDE, COUNTRYSIDE
Answer Key and Teaching Notes

9. Antonym of *urban*.
Change 1 letter.

r u r a l

8. A large work of art on a wall.
Change 2 letters.

m u r a l

7. Dark and cloudy.
Change 1 letter, then add 1.

m u r k y

6. To wait secretly.
Change 1 letter.
In pairs, have students repeat and complete, "One place that would be really creepy to lurk is…"

l u r k

⭐ **5. An inhabitant of Turkey.**
Change 1 letter.
Point out where Turkey is located on a map.

T u r k

t u r n

4. To rotate.
Take away 2 letters, then add 1.

⭐ **3. To agitate or mix.**
Add 2 letters.

c h u r n

2. A type of vase.
Take away 1 letter.
Teach students that a common use for an urn is to store someone's ashes when he or she passes away and is cremated.

u r n

1. To overcook something.
Take away 1 letter, then rearrange.

Start Here

b u r n

u r b a n

Urban _____ areas are more densely populated than _____ rural _____ areas and can include towns and cities.

Read each clue and write the answer in the blanks.
Use the first and last words to fill in the sentence under the ladder.

HINT! Words with a ⭐ are more challenging!

SOCIAL STUDIES

ASKING FOR DIRECTIONS

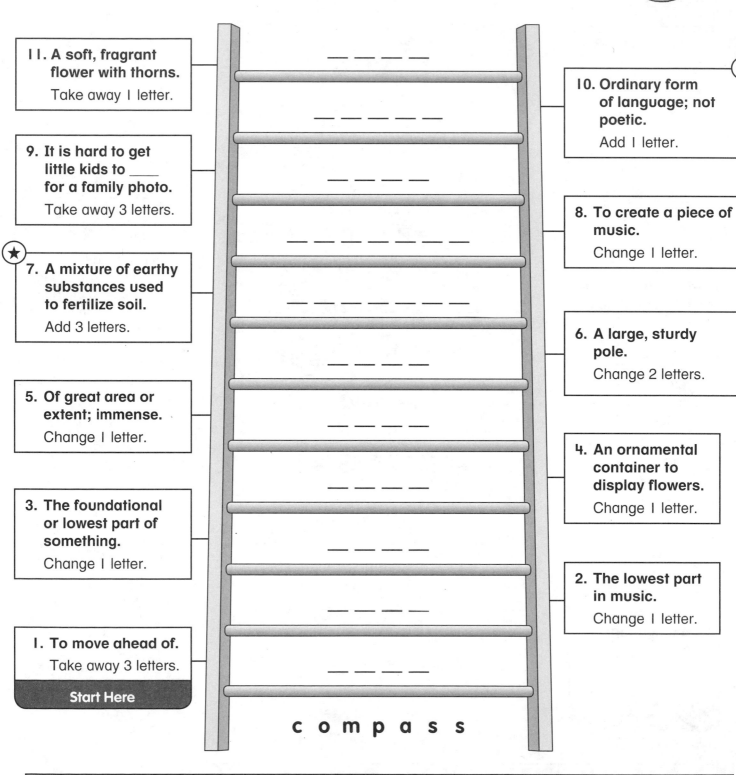

11. **A soft, fragrant flower with thorns.**
Take away 1 letter.

— — — — —

10. Ordinary form of language; not poetic. ⭐
Add 1 letter.

— — — — — —

9. It is hard to get little kids to ____ for a family photo.
Take away 3 letters.

— — — —

8. To create a piece of music.
Change 1 letter.

— — — — — — —

⭐
7. A mixture of earthy substances used to fertilize soil.
Add 3 letters.

— — — — — — —

6. A large, sturdy pole.
Change 2 letters.

— — — —

5. Of great area or extent; immense.
Change 1 letter.

— — — —

4. An ornamental container to display flowers.
Change 1 letter.

— — — —

3. The foundational or lowest part of something.
Change 1 letter.

— — — —

2. The lowest part in music.
Change 1 letter.

1. To move ahead of.
Take away 3 letters.

Start Here

— — — —

c o m p a s s

A _____ _____ is a circle showing the principal directions on a map.

ASKING FOR DIRECTIONS
Answer Key and Teaching Notes

11. A soft, fragrant flower with thorns.
Take away 1 letter.

r o s e

10. Ordinary form of language; not poetic. ⭐
Add 1 letter.

p r o s e

9. It is hard to get little kids to ____ for a family photo.
Take away 3 letters.

p o s e

8. To create a piece of music.
Change 1 letter.
Have students determine the number of syllables (vowel sounds) in the word.

c o m p o s e

⭐ **7. A mixture of earthy substances used to fertilize soil.**
Add 3 letters.

c o m p o s t

6. A large, sturdy pole.
Change 2 letters.

p o s t

5. Of great area or extent; immense.
Change 1 letter.

v a s t

4. An ornamental container to display flowers.
Change 1 letter.

v a s e

3. The foundational or lowest part of something.
Change 1 letter.
Homophone: *bass*, a musical instrument.

b a s e

2. The lowest part in music.
Change 1 letter.
Homograph: (noun) a type of fish.

b a s s

1. To move ahead of.
Take away 3 letters.

p a s s

Start Here

c o m p a s s

A _____ compass _____ _____ rose _____ is a circle showing the principal directions on a map.

Name _____

Read each clue and write the answer in the blanks.
Use the first and last words to fill in the sentence under the ladder.

SOCIAL STUDIES

MORE OR LESS

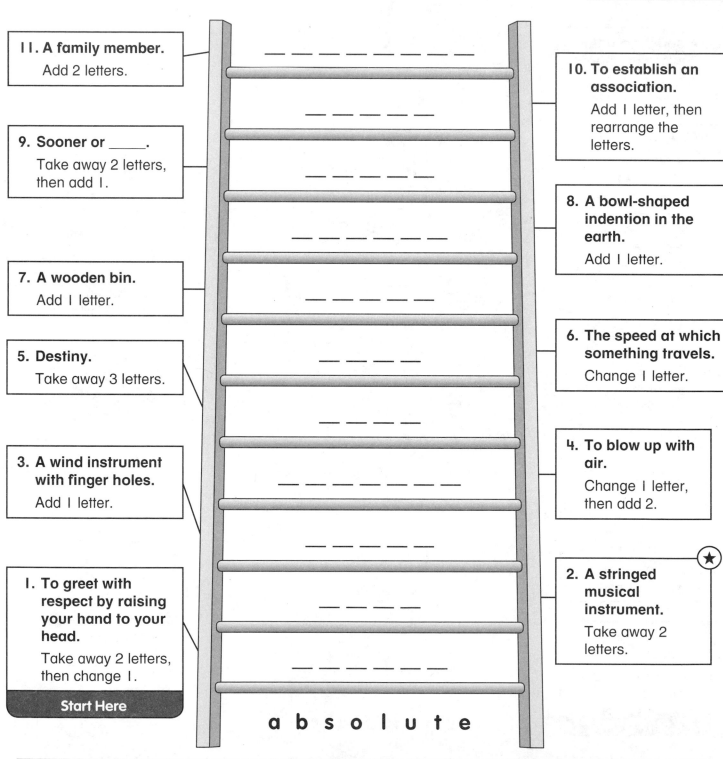

11. A family member.
Add 2 letters.

— — — — — — — —

10. To establish an association.
Add 1 letter, then rearrange the letters.

— — — — — —

9. Sooner or ____.
Take away 2 letters, then add 1.

— — — — —

8. A bowl-shaped indention in the earth.
Add 1 letter.

— — — — — — —

7. A wooden bin.
Add 1 letter.

— — — — — —

6. The speed at which something travels.
Change 1 letter.

— — — —

5. Destiny.
Take away 3 letters.

— — — —

4. To blow up with air.
Change 1 letter, then add 2.

— — — — — — — —

3. A wind instrument with finger holes.
Add 1 letter.

— — — — — —

⭐
2. A stringed musical instrument.
Take away 2 letters.

— — — —

1. To greet with respect by raising your hand to your head.
Take away 2 letters, then change 1.

Start Here

— — — — — — —

a b s o l u t e

_____ location is the position of something in relation to another landmark, while _____ location is the fixed position described with coordinates of latitude and longitude.

MORE OR LESS
Answer Key and Teaching Notes

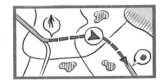

11. A family member.
Add 2 letters.

r e l a t i v e

10. To establish an association.
Add 1 letter, then rearrange the letters.

r e l a t e

9. Sooner or _____.
Take away 2 letters, then add 1.

l a t e r

8. A bowl-shaped indention in the earth.
Add 1 letter.

c r a t e r

7. A wooden bin.
Add 1 letter.

c r a t e

6. The speed at which something travels.
Change 1 letter.
Multiple meaning word: a certain fee charged for something.

5. Destiny.
Take away 3 letters.
Figure of speech: *tempt fate*, to do something that you know is risky.

r a t e

f a t e

3. A wind instrument with finger holes.
Add 1 letter.

i n f l a t e

4. To blow up with air.
Change 1 letter, then add 2.

f l u t e

1. To greet with respect by raising your hand to your head.
Take away 2 letters, then change 1.

Start Here

l u t e

⭐
2. A stringed musical instrument.
Take away 2 letters.
Show students a digital picture of a lute.

s a l u t e

a b s o l u t e

_____Relative_____ location is the position of something in relation to another landmark, while _____absolute_____ location is the fixed position described with coordinates of latitude and longitude.

Name _____

Read each clue and write the answer in the blanks.
Use the first and last words to fill in the sentence under the ladder.

HINT! Words with a ★ are more challenging!

SOCIAL STUDIES

WHAT ARE YOUR SOURCES?

11. Red, yellow, and blue are ___ colors.
Add 3 letters.

9. The edge of a cup or a bowl.
Change 1 letter.

★ **7. 500 sheets of paper.**
Change 1 letter.

5. To step or walk.
Change 1 letter.

3. To pay attention to or take care of.
Change 1 letter.

1. After the first.
Take away 3 letters.

Start Here

10. Proper. ★
Add 1 letter.

8. To run forcefully into something.
Take away 1 letter.

6. To understand written words.
Take away 1 letter.

4. A popular style.
Add 1 letter.

2. To transmit a signal.
Take away 2 letters.

s e c o n d a r y

A _____ resource is a firsthand account of history, while a _____
resource is an interpretation or analysis of a primary source.

WHAT ARE YOUR SOURCES?

Answer Key and Teaching Notes

11. Red, yellow, and blue are ____ colors.

Add 3 letters.

p r i m a r y

10. Proper. ★

Add 1 letter.

p r i m

9. The edge of a cup or a bowl.

Change 1 letter.

r i m

8. To run forcefully into something.

Take away 1 letter.

Multiple meaning word: a male sheep.

r a m

★ **7. 500 sheets of paper.**

Change 1 letter.

Show students an image of a ream of paper, or a real one!

r e a m

6. To understand written words.

Take away 1 letter.

r e a d

5. To step or walk.

Change 1 letter.

t r e a d

4. A popular style.

Add 1 letter.

In pairs, have students repeat and complete, "One current trend I really like is…"

t r e n d

3. To pay attention to or take care of.

Change 1 letter.

t e n d

2. To transmit a signal.

Take away 2 letters.

s e n d

1. After the first.

Take away 3 letters.

Start Here

s e c o n d

s e c o n d a r y

A ____primary____ resource is a firsthand account of history, while a ____secondary____ resource is an interpretation or analysis of a primary source.

TIP! You may want to offer students some extra support for these more challenging words, marked with a ★.

Name _____

Read each clue and write the answer in the blanks.
Use the first and last words to fill in the sentence under the ladder.

HINT! Words with a (★) are more challenging!

SCIENCE

STEP BY STEP

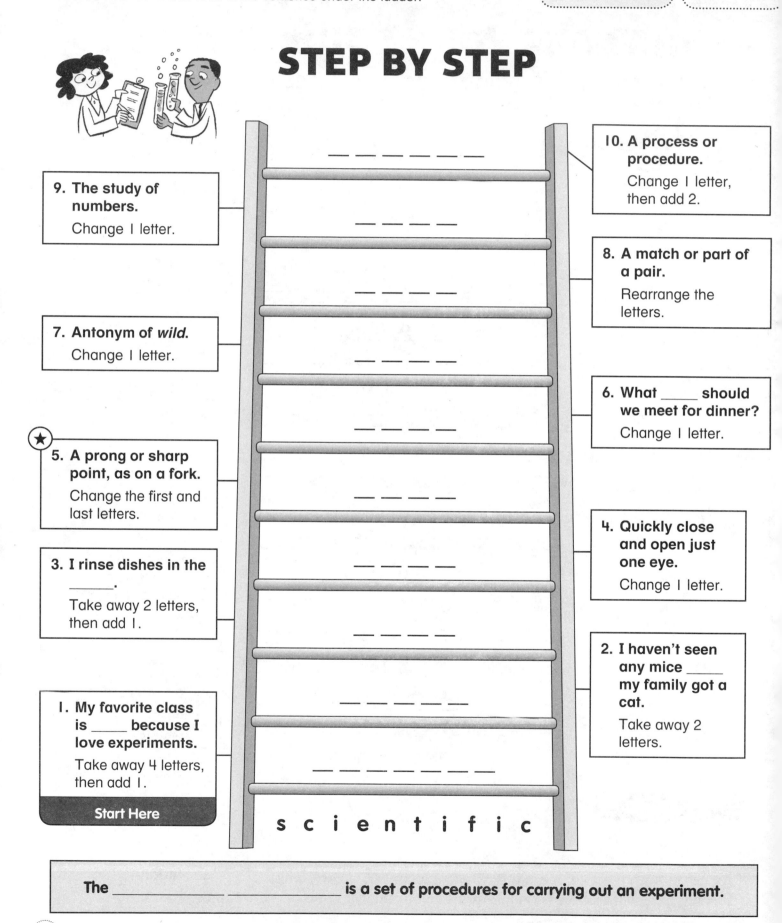

10. A process or procedure.
Change 1 letter, then add 2.

9. The study of numbers.
Change 1 letter.

8. A match or part of a pair.
Rearrange the letters.

7. Antonym of *wild*.
Change 1 letter.

6. What _____ should we meet for dinner?
Change 1 letter.

★

5. A prong or sharp point, as on a fork.
Change the first and last letters.

4. Quickly close and open just one eye.
Change 1 letter.

3. I rinse dishes in the _____.
Take away 2 letters, then add 1.

2. I haven't seen any mice _____ my family got a cat.
Take away 2 letters.

1. My favorite class is _____ because I love experiments.
Take away 4 letters, then add 1.

Start Here

s c i e n t i f i c

The _____ _____ is a set of procedures for carrying out an experiment.

STEP BY STEP
Answer Key and Teaching Notes

m e t h o d

m a t h

m a t e

t a m e

t i m e

t i n e

w i n k

s i n k

s i n c e

s c i e n c e

s c i e n t i f i c

Start Here

9. The study of numbers.
Change 1 letter.

7. Antonym of *wild*.
Change 1 letter.

★ **5. A prong or sharp point, as on a fork.**
Change the first and last letters.

3. I rinse dishes in the _____.
Take away 2 letters, then add 1.
Multiple meaning word: to fall deeper in water.

1. My favorite class is _____ because I love experiments.
Take away 4 letters, then add 1.
In pairs, have students share their favorite science topic.

10. A process or procedure.
Change 1 letter, then add 2.

8. A match or part of a pair.
Rearrange the letters.

6. What _____ should we meet for dinner?
Change 1 letter.
Multiple meaning word: to keep track of how long it takes someone to do something, as in "to time the race."

4. Quickly close and open just one eye.
Change 1 letter.

2. I haven't seen any mice _____ my family got a cat.
Take away 2 letters.

The __scientific__ __method__ is a set of procedures for carrying out an experiment.

Name _____

Read each clue and write the answer in the blanks.
Use the first and last words to fill in the sentence under the ladder.

HINT! Words with a ★ are more challenging!

SCIENCE

TAKE YOUR BEST GUESS

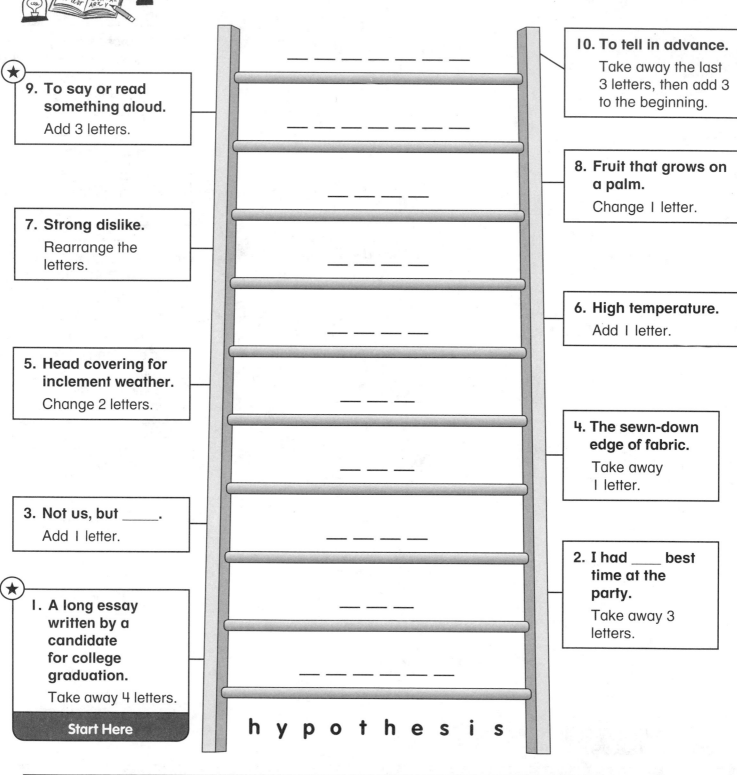

★ **9. To say or read something aloud.**
Add 3 letters.

7. Strong dislike.
Rearrange the letters.

5. Head covering for inclement weather.
Change 2 letters.

3. Not us, but _____.
Add 1 letter.

★ **1. A long essay written by a candidate for college graduation.**
Take away 4 letters.

Start Here

10. To tell in advance.
Take away the last 3 letters, then add 3 to the beginning.

8. Fruit that grows on a palm.
Change 1 letter.

6. High temperature.
Add 1 letter.

4. The sewn-down edge of fabric.
Take away 1 letter.

2. I had _____ best time at the party.
Take away 3 letters.

h y p o t h e s i s

With a _____, scientists _____ the results of an experiment.

146

TAKE YOUR BEST GUESS
Answer Key and Teaching Notes

Ladder (top to bottom):

p r e d i c t

d i c t a t e

d a t e

h a t e

h e a t

h a t

h e m

t h e m

t h e

t h e s i s

h y p o t h e s i s

Start Here

---

10. To tell in advance.

Take away the last 3 letters, then add 3 to the beginning.

In pairs, have students share predictions about an upcoming event.

★ **9. To say or read something aloud.**

Add 3 letters.

8. Fruit that grows on a palm.

Change 1 letter.

Multiple meaning word: a specific day of the month and year, such as July 4, 2019.

7. Strong dislike.

Rearrange the letters.

Have students come up with strategies for reducing hateful actions between groups of people.

6. High temperature.

Add 1 letter.

5. Head covering for inclement weather.

Change 2 letters.

4. The sewn-down edge of fabric.

Take away 1 letter.

3. Not us, but _____.

Add 1 letter.

2. I had _____ best time at the party.

Take away 3 letters.

★ **1. A long essay written by a candidate for college graduation.**

Take away 4 letters.

With a _hypothesis_ **, scientists** _predict_ **the results of an experiment.**

Name _____

Read each clue and write the answer in the blanks.
Use the first and last words to fill in the sentence under the ladder.

SCIENCE

DIFFUSING DROPLETS

8. H₂O.
   Add 1 letter, then rearrange.

   _ _ _ _ _

7. The car was going at a ____ of 50 mph.
   Change 1 letter.

   _ _ _ _

6. Doing something by habit or routine. ⭐
   Change 1 letter.

   _ _ _ _ _

5. A fragrant flower.
   Change 1 letter.

   _ _ _ _

4. To assume a particular attitude or position in order to be photographed.
   Change 1 letter.

   _ _ _ _

3. Fancy or luxurious. ⭐
   Take away 1 letter, then change 1.

   _ _ _ _

2. A group of people with a common characteristic or purpose. ⭐
   Change 1 letter, then add 1.

   _ _ _ _ _

1. A moist, spongy plant that often grows on tree trunks.
   Take away 3 letters.

   Start Here

   _ _ _ _

o s m o s i s

_____ is the diffusion or passing through of _____ molecules through a membrane.

TIP! You may want to offer students some extra support for these more challenging words, marked with a ★.

DIFFUSING DROPLETS
Answer Key and Teaching Notes

w a t e r

8. H₂O.
Add 1 letter, then rearrange.

7. The car was going at a ____ of 50 mph.
Change 1 letter.

r a t e

6. Doing something by habit or routine. ★
Change 1 letter.
Homophone: *wrote*, past tense of *write*.

r o t e

5. A fragrant flower.
Change 1 letter.
Multiple meaning word: past tense of *rise*, to move from a lower position to a higher one.

r o s e

4. To assume a particular attitude or position in order to be photographed.
Change 1 letter.
Have students get up and demonstrate a favorite pose.

p o s e

3. Fancy or luxurious. ★
Take away 1 letter, then change 1.

p o s h

2. A group of people with a common characteristic or purpose. ★
Change 1 letter, then add 1.

p o s s e

1. A moist, spongy plant that often grows on tree trunks.
Take away 3 letters.

Start Here

m o s s

o s m o s i s

____Osmosis____ is the diffusion or passing through of ____water____ molecules through a membrane.

Read each clue and write the answer in the blanks.
Use the first and last words to fill in the sentence under the ladder.

SUNSCREEN

11. Onions have more than one _____.
Rearrange the letters.

— — — — — —

10. To pass on.
Change 1 letter.

— — — — —

9. To calm down.
Add 2 letters.

— — — — —

8. Laid back, not rigid. ★
Change 1 letter.

— — —

7. Money paid to the government.
Take away 2 letters, then change 1.

— — —

6. Poisonous. ★
Add 3 letters.

— — — — —

5. Beast of burden.
Change 1 letter.

— —

4. Antonym of off.
Take away 1 letter.

— —

3. A word for 2,000 pounds.
Take away 1 letter.

— — —

2. The quality of a sound.
Change 1 letter.

— — — —

1. A designated area.
Take away 1 letter.

Start Here

— — — —

o z o n e

The _____ _____ is a part of the earth's atmosphere that absorbs ultraviolet radiation from the sun before it reaches the surface of the earth.

SUNSCREEN
Answer Key and Teaching Notes

l a y e r

r e l a y

r e l a x

l a x

t a x

t o x i c

o x

o n

t o n

t o n e

z o n e

o z o n e

Start Here

11. Onions have more than one _____.
Rearrange the letters.

9. To calm down.
Add 2 letters.

7. Money paid to the government.
Take away 2 letters, then change 1.

5. Beast of burden.
Change 1 letter.
Discuss the spelling of the plural form of the word (*oxen*).

3. A word for 2,000 pounds.
Take away 1 letter.
Have students list synonyms for *ton* (*a lot, many, numerous*).

1. A designated area.
Take away 1 letter.

10. To pass on.
Change 1 letter.
Homograph: (noun) a type of race done as a team, with one person at a time passing a baton.

8. Laid back, not rigid. ★
Change 1 letter.

6. Poisonous. ★
Add 3 letters.

4. Antonym of *off*.
Take away 1 letter.

2. The quality of a sound.
Change 1 letter.

The ____ozone____ ____layer____ is a part of the earth's atmosphere that absorbs ultraviolet radiation from the sun before it reaches the surface of the earth.

Read each clue and write the answer in the blanks.
Use the first and last words to fill in the sentence under the ladder.

SCIENCE

WILD WINDS

9. Vortex of strong wind.
Add 3 letters to the end.

— — — — — — — — —

8. A synonym for *ripped*.
Change 1 letter.

— — — —

7. A yellow vegetable that grows on a cob.
Change 1 letter.

— — — —

6. I needed new clothes because my old ones were ____ out.
Change 1 letter.

— — — —

5. My baby brother was ____ this morning.
Change 1 letter.

— — — —

4. A person who is not interesting. ★
Change 1 letter.

— — — —

3. The very center of an object.
Change 1 letter.

— — — —

2. To show concern.
Change 1 letter.

— — — —

1. My grandpa needs a ____ to help him walk.
Take away 5 letters.

Start Here

— — — —

h u r r i c a n e

A _____ forms over land, while a _____ is much larger and forms over water.

WILD WINDS
Answer Key and Teaching Notes

9. Vortex of strong wind.

Add 3 letters to the end.

Have students count the number of syllables (vowel sounds) in the word.

7. A yellow vegetable that grows on a cob.

Change 1 letter.

5. My baby brother was _____ this morning.

Change 1 letter.

3. The very center of an object.

Change 1 letter.

Multiple meaning word: the part of an apple that contains seeds.

1. My grandpa needs a _____ to help him walk.

Take away 5 letters.

Start Here

t o r n a d o

t _ o r n

c _ o r n

w _ o r n

b o r n

b o r e

c _ o r e

c a r e

c a n e

h u r r i c a n e

8. A synonym for *ripped*.

Change 1 letter.

Have students list synonyms for *torn* (*broken, damaged, ripped, severed*).

6. I needed new clothes because my old ones were _____ out.

Change 1 letter.

⭐ **4. A person who is not interesting.**

Change 1 letter.

Multiple meaning word: to drill a hole. Homophone: *boar*, a wild pig.

2. To show concern.

Change 1 letter.

A _____**tornado**_____ forms over land, while a _____**hurricane**_____ is much larger and forms over water.

Name _____

Read each clue and write the answer in the blanks.
Use the first and last words to fill in the sentence under the ladder.

SCIENCE

EXTENDED FAMILY

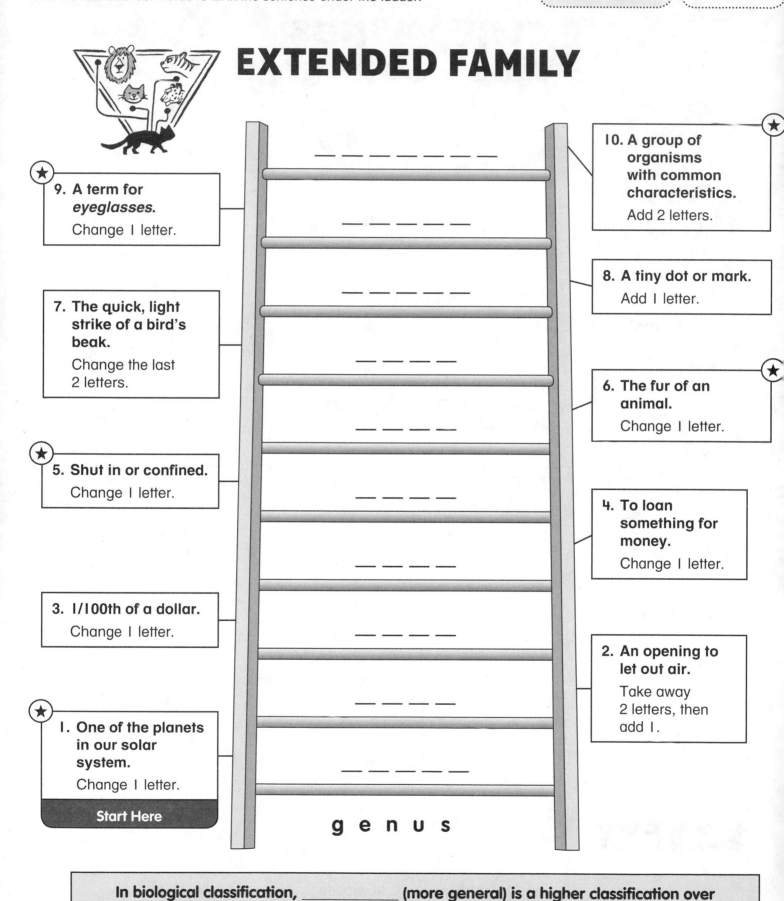

⭐ 9. A term for *eyeglasses*.
Change 1 letter.

7. The quick, light strike of a bird's beak.
Change the last 2 letters.

⭐ 5. Shut in or confined.
Change 1 letter.

3. 1/100th of a dollar.
Change 1 letter.

⭐ 1. One of the planets in our solar system.
Change 1 letter.

Start Here

⭐ 10. A group of organisms with common characteristics.
Add 2 letters.

8. A tiny dot or mark.
Add 1 letter.

⭐ 6. The fur of an animal.
Change 1 letter.

4. To loan something for money.
Change 1 letter.

2. An opening to let out air.
Take away 2 letters, then add 1.

g e n u s

In biological classification, _____ (more general) is a higher classification over _____ (more specific).

EXTENDED FAMILY
Answer Key and Teaching Notes

10. A group of organisms with common characteristics. ★

Add 2 letters.

Give an example of scientific nomenclature: the domesticated dog is *Canis* (genus) *familiaris* (species).

9. A term for *eyeglasses*. ★

Change 1 letter.

7. The quick, light strike of a bird's beak.

Change the last 2 letters.

Multiple meaning word: a measure of 8 quarts.

8. A tiny dot or mark.

Add 1 letter.

5. Shut in or confined. ★

Change 1 letter.

6. The fur of an animal. ★

Change 1 letter.

Multiple meaning word: to throw something at someone.

3. 1/100th of a dollar.

Change 1 letter.

4. To loan something for money.

Change 1 letter.

1. One of the planets in our solar system. ★

Change 1 letter.

Start Here

2. An opening to let out air.

Take away 2 letters, then add 1.

s p e c i e s

s p e c s

s p e c k

p e c k

p e l t

p e n t

r e n t

c e n t

v e n t

V e n u s

g e n u s

In biological classification, __genus__ (more general) is a higher classification over __species__ (more specific).

Read each clue and write the answer in the blanks.
Use the first and last words to fill in the sentence under the ladder.

HINT! Words with a ⭐ are more challenging!

SCIENCE

MAKERS & TAKERS

11. A person who makes a product.
Add 4 letters.

— — — — — — — —

10. To poke or jab.
Change 1 letter, then rearrange.

9. A small body of water.
Change the first 2 letters.

— — — —

— — — —

8. A musical group.
Change 1 letter.

7. A place to keep money.
Change 1 letter.

— — — —

— — — —

6. The _____ beds were stacked on top of each other.
Add 1 letter.

5. A hot dog comes in a ___.
Change 1 letter.

— — — —

— — —

4. The star our planet revolves around.
Change 1 letter.

3. To add up.
Take away 3 letters.

— — —

— — — — — —

2. To start again.
Take away 1 letter.

1. To assume.
Take away 1 letter, then change the first 3.

Start Here

— — — — — — — —

c o n s u m e r

A _____ generates its food, while a _____ does not produce anything, but instead eats producers or other consumers.

MAKERS & TAKERS
Answer Key and Teaching Notes

11. A person who makes a product.
Add 4 letters.

9. A small body of water.
Change the first 2 letters.
Have students name other bodies of water (*ocean, river, sea*).

7. A place to keep money.
Change 1 letter.

5. A hot dog comes in a ___.
Change 1 letter.

3. To add up.
Take away 3 letters.
Homophone: *some*, neither all nor none.

1. To assume.
Take away 1 letter, then change the first 3.

Start Here

p r o d u c e r

p r o d

p o n d

b a n d

b a n k

b u n k

b u n

s u n

s u m

r e s u m e

p r e s u m e

c o n s u m e r

★ 10. To poke or jab.
Change 1 letter, then rearrange.

8. A musical group.
Change 1 letter.
Multiple meaning word: to *band together* means to "bring together."

6. The _____ beds were stacked on top of each other.
Add 1 letter.

4. The star our planet revolves around.
Change 1 letter.

2. To start again.
Take away 1 letter.

A ___producer___ generates its food, while a ___consumer___ does not produce anything, but instead eats producers or other consumers.

157

Name _____

Read each clue and write the answer in the blanks.
Use the first and last words to fill in the sentence under the ladder.

HINT! Words with a ★ are more challenging!

SCIENCE

ACHOO!

11. I planted a ___ to grow a tree.
Change 1 letter.

9. To connect metal by melting.
Change the first letter, then rearrange.

7. The color of the clear sky.
Change 1 letter, then rearrange.

5. A type of bird that lives near the water.
Take away 2 letters.

★ **3. A simple machine used to move or lift heavy objects.**
Add 2 letters.

★ **1. To take a survey.**
Take away 2 letters.

Start Here

10. A troublesome plant.
Change 1 letter.

8. The wind ___ relentlessly.
Take away 1 letter, then add 1 to the end.

6. A large male animal with horns.
Change 1 letter.

★ **4. A ravine or trench.**
Change 1 letter.

2. To move toward yourself.
Change 1 letter.

p o l l e n

Fine and powdery, _____ travels by wind or insect from a flowering plant to fertilize the _____ of another plant.

TIP! You may want to offer students some extra support for these more challenging words, marked with a ★.

ACHOO!
Answer Key and Teaching Notes

11. I planted a ___ to grow a tree.
Change 1 letter.

s e e d

w e e d

10. A troublesome plant.
Change 1 letter.

9. To connect metal by melting.
Change the first letter, then rearrange.

w e l d

7. The color of the clear sky.
Change 1 letter, then rearrange.

b l e w

8. The wind ___ relentlessly.
Take away 1 letter, then add 1 to the end.
Homophone: *blue*, a color.

b l u e

5. A type of bird that lives near the water.
Take away 2 letters.
In pairs, have students list as many different birds as they can.

b u l l

g u l l

6. A large male animal with horns.
Change 1 letter.

g u l l e y

★ **4. A ravine or trench.**
Change 1 letter.

★ **3. A simple machine used to move or lift heavy objects.**
Add 2 letters.

p u l l e y

p u l l

2. To move toward yourself.
Change 1 letter.
Have students list synonyms for *pull* (*tug, drag, yank*).

★ **1. To take a survey.**
Take away 2 letters.

Start Here

p o l l

p o l l e n

Fine and powdery, _____**pollen**_____ travels by wind or insect from a flowering plant to fertilize the _____**seed**_____ of another plant.

Read each clue and write the answer in the blanks.
Use the first and last words to fill in the sentence under the ladder.

HINT! Words with a ⭐ are more challenging!

SCIENCE

ITTY-BITTY INFECTIONS

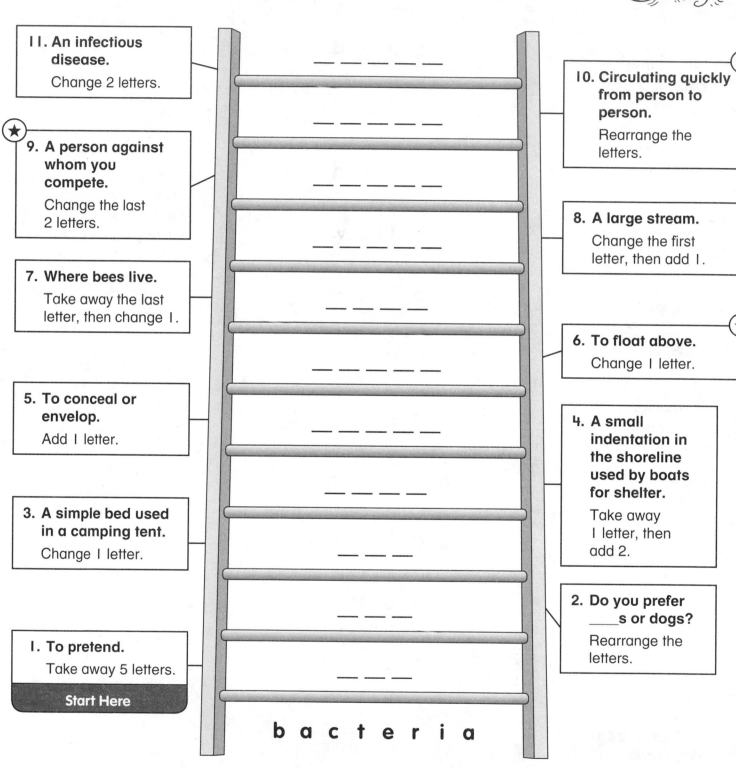

11. An infectious disease.
Change 2 letters.

9. A person against whom you compete. ⭐
Change the last 2 letters.

7. Where bees live.
Take away the last letter, then change 1.

5. To conceal or envelop.
Add 1 letter.

3. A simple bed used in a camping tent.
Change 1 letter.

1. To pretend.
Take away 5 letters.

Start Here

10. Circulating quickly from person to person. ⭐
Rearrange the letters.

8. A large stream.
Change the first letter, then add 1.

6. To float above. ⭐
Change 1 letter.

4. A small indentation in the shoreline used by boats for shelter.
Take away 1 letter, then add 2.

2. Do you prefer ____s or dogs?
Rearrange the letters.

b a c t e r i a

Some illnesses, like the common cold, are caused by a _____; some illnesses are caused by _____.

TIP! You may want to offer students some extra support for these more challenging words, marked with a ⭐.

ITTY-BITTY INFECTIONS
Answer Key and Teaching Notes

11. An infectious disease.
Change 2 letters.

⭐ **9. A person against whom you compete.**
Change the last 2 letters.

7. Where bees live.
Take away the last letter, then change 1.

5. To conceal or envelop.
Add 1 letter.

3. A simple bed used in a camping tent.
Change 1 letter.
Have students list other things you can sleep on besides a cot (*bed, sleeping bag, blow-up mattress, couch*).

1. To pretend.
Take away 5 letters.

Start Here

v i r u s

v i r a l

r i v a l

r i v e r

h i v e

h o v e r

c o v e r

c o v e

c o t

c a t

a c t

b a c t e r i a

⭐ **10. Circulating quickly from person to person.**
Rearrange the letters.

8. A large stream.
Change the first letter, then add 1.

⭐ **6. To float above.**
Change 1 letter.

4. A small indentation in the shoreline used by boats for shelter.
Take away 1 letter, then add 2.

2. Do you prefer ____s or dogs?
Rearrange the letters.

Some illnesses, like the common cold, are caused by a __virus__; some illnesses are caused by __bacteria__.

Name _____

Read each clue and write the answer in the blanks.
Use the first and last words to fill in the sentence under the ladder.

SIT OR STAND

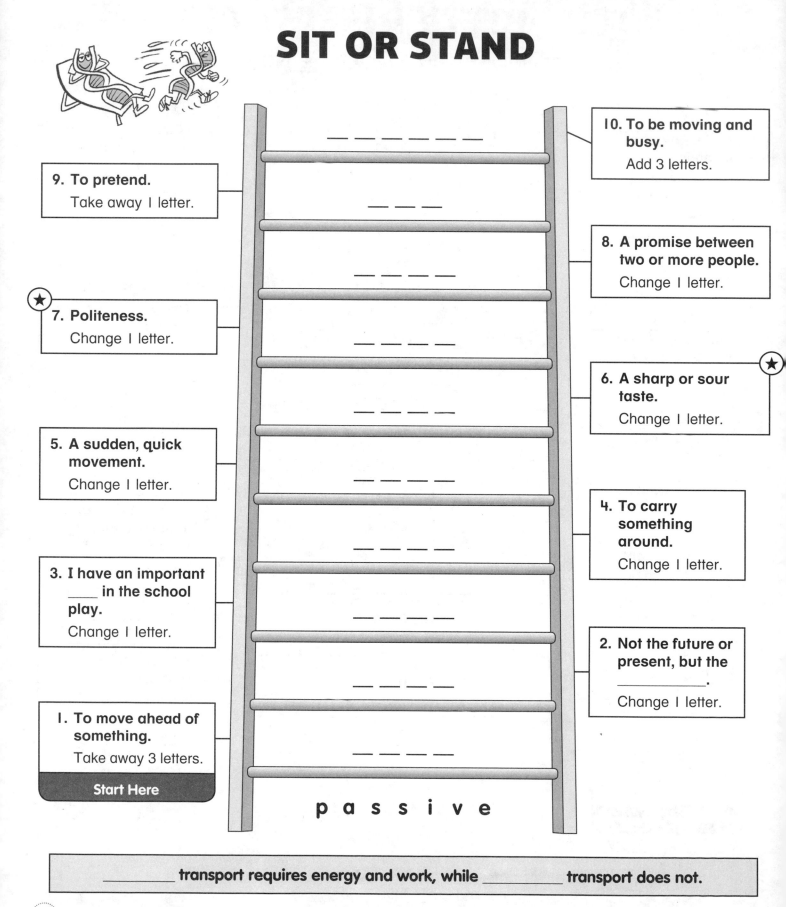

10. To be moving and busy.
Add 3 letters.

_ _ _ _ _ _

9. To pretend.
Take away I letter.

_ _ _

8. A promise between two or more people.
Change I letter.

_ _ _ _

★ **7. Politeness.**
Change I letter.

_ _ _ _

★ **6. A sharp or sour taste.**
Change I letter.

_ _ _ _

5. A sudden, quick movement.
Change I letter.

_ _ _ _

4. To carry something around.
Change I letter.

_ _ _ _

3. I have an important ____ in the school play.
Change I letter.

_ _ _ _

2. Not the future or present, but the _____.
Change I letter.

_ _ _ _

I. To move ahead of something.
Take away 3 letters.

Start Here

_ _ _ _

p a s s i v e

_____ transport requires energy and work, while _____ transport does not.

SIT OR STAND
Answer Key and Teaching Notes

a c t i v e

10. To be moving and busy.
Add 3 letters.

9. To pretend.
Take away 1 letter.
Multiple meaning word: a thing done, or a deed.

a c t

8. A promise between two or more people.
Change 1 letter.
Have students list synonyms of *pact* (*agreement, deal, understanding*).

p a c t

★ **7. Politeness.**
Change 1 letter.

t a c t

t a r t

★ **6. A sharp or sour taste.**
Change 1 letter.
Multiple meaning word: a round pastry.

5. A sudden, quick movement.
Change 1 letter.

d a r t

c a r t

4. To carry something around.
Change 1 letter.

3. I have an important ____ in the school play.
Change 1 letter.

p a r t

2. Not the future or present, but the _____.
Change 1 letter.
Homophone: *passed*, past tense of *pass*.

p a s t

1. To move ahead of something.
Take away 3 letters.

Start Here

p a s s

p a s s i v e

<u>Active</u> transport requires energy and work, while <u>passive</u> transport does not.

Read each clue and write the answer in the blanks.
Use the first and last words to fill in the sentence under the ladder.

HINT! Words with a ★ are more challenging!

SCIENCE

STAYING ACTIVE

9. Out of sight.
Add 3 letters.

— — — — — — —

8. A bear often hibernates in a ___.
Take away 1 letter.

— — —

7. The accident left a small ___ in the car.
Take away 1 letter.

— — — — —

6. One penny.
Take away 2 letters, then add 1.

— — — —

5. To repeat a series of words, often as a group.
Change 1 letter.

— — — — — —

4. A type of graph.
Add 1 letter.

— — — — — —

3. I put lots of snacks in the grocery ___.
Take away 1 letter, then rearrange the letters.

— — — — —

2. To act in response to another action.
Add 2 letters.

1. A section, or part, of a play.
Take away 3 letters.

Start Here

— — —

a c t i v e

A virus can either be _____ and go into action immediately, or _____ and not be active for a while.

TIP! You may want to offer students some extra support for these more challenging words, marked with a ⊛.

STAYING ACTIVE
Answer Key and Teaching Notes

9. Out of sight.
Add 3 letters.

h i d d e n

8. A bear often hibernates in a ___.
Take away 1 letter.

d e n

7. The accident left a small ___ in the car.
Take away 1 letter.

d e n t

6. One penny.
Take away 2 letters, then add 1.
Homophone: *sent*, past tense of *send*.

c e n t

5. To repeat a series of words, often as a group.
Change 1 letter.

c h a n t

4. A type of graph.
Add 1 letter.

c h a r t

3. I put lots of snacks in the grocery ___.
Take away 1 letter, then rearrange the letters.
Multiple meaning word: to carry around.

c a r t

2. To act in response to another action.
Add 2 letters.
Discuss how *re-* means to do something again (as in *redo, reappear, replay, reform*).

r e a c t

1. A section, or part, of a play.
Take away 3 letters.

a c t

Start Here

a c t i v e

A virus can either be ___active___ and go into action immediately, or ___hidden___ and not be active for a while.

Name _____

Read each clue and write the answer in the blanks.
Use the first and last words to fill in the sentence under the ladder.

HINT! Words with a ⭐ are more challenging!

SCIENCE

PASS IT ALONG

11. The opposite of *dominant*.
Add 3 letters.

9. To admit to doing something wrong.
Take away the *h*, then add 3 letters.

7. There was gold in the treasure ____.
Take away 1 letter, then add 2.

5. To stroke softly.
Change 2 letters.

3. The most important part of something.
Take away 1 letter, then rearrange the remaining letters.

1. A tile in a game where you match patterns of dots.
Take away 3 letters, then add 1.

Start Here

10. A time of day when you play at school.
Take away 3 letters, then add 2.

8. A board game with a king, queen, and pawns.
Change 1 letter.

6. What an exterminator gets rid of.
Add 1 letter.

4. A tool used to cook with.
Take away 2 letters, then add 1.

⭐

2. A chemical compound that helps build protein.
Take away 2 letters, then add 1.

d o m i n a n t

A _____ trait can be created from just one parent, while a _____ trait must come from both parents.

TIP! You may want to offer students some extra support for these more challenging words, marked with a ★.

PASS IT ALONG

Answer Key and Teaching Notes

11. The opposite of *dominant*.
Add 3 letters.
Have students count the number of syllables (vowel sounds) in the word.

r e c e s s i v e

10. A time of day when you play at school.
Take away 3 letters, then add 2.

r e c e s s

9. To admit to doing something wrong.
Take away the *h*, then add 3 letters.

c o n f e s s

8. A board game with a king, queen, and pawns.
Change 1 letter.

c h e s s

7. There was gold in the treasure _____.
Take away 1 letter, then add 2.

c h e s t

6. What an exterminator gets rid of.
Add 1 letter.

p e s t

5. To stroke softly.
Change 2 letters.
Multiple meaning word: an animal kept in the house.

p e t

4. A tool used to cook with.
Take away 2 letters, then add 1.
Figure of speech: *pan out*, when something works out.

p a n

3. The most important part of something.
Take away 1 letter, then rearrange the remaining letters.

m a i n

2. A chemical compound that helps build protein. ★
Take away 2 letters, then add 1.

a m i n o

1. A tile in a game where you match patterns of dots.
Take away 3 letters, then add 1.

d o m i n o

Start Here

d o m i n a n t

A dominant trait can be created from just one parent, while a recessive trait must come from both parents.

Read each clue and write the answer in the blanks.
Use the first and last words to fill in the sentence under the ladder.

HINT! Words with a (★) are more challenging!

SCIENCE

BUILDING BLOCKS

11. Something with a sour taste.

Take away 2 letters.

9. The cattle lived on a _____.

Take away the first letter, then change the vowel.

★ 7. A miserable or despicable person.

Take away 1 letter, then add 2.

★ 5. A crank or handle of a revolving machine.

Change 1 letter.

3. In bowling, you want to knock all the ___ over.

Change 1 letter.

1. Subtraction symbol: ____ sign.

Take away the first and last letters, then add 2.

Start Here

_ _ _ _ _

_ _ _ _ _ _

_ _ _ _ _

_ _ _ _ _ _

_ _ _ _ _ _

_ _ _ _ _

_ _ _ _ _

_ _ _ _ _

_ _ _ _

_ _ _ _

_ _ _ _ _

a m i n o

★ 10. Spoiled or rotten.

Take away the last letter, then add 2.

8. A tool used to loosen a bolt.

Change 1 letter.

6. The _____ rode on her broomstick.

Change 1 letter.

4. A small amount. I added a ___ of salt to the recipe.

Take away the last letter, then add 2.

2. Containers in which you store things.

Take away 2 letters, then add 1.

An _____ _____ is an organic molecule and a building block of protein.

TIP! You may want to offer students some extra support for these more challenging words, marked with a ★.

BUILDING BLOCKS
Answer Key and Teaching Notes

11. Something with a sour taste.

Take away 2 letters.

a c i d

10. Spoiled or rotten. ★

Take away the last letter, then add 2.

r a n c i d

9. The cattle lived on a _____.

Take away the first letter, then change the vowel.

Multiple meaning word: a kind of salad dressing.

r a n c h

8. A tool used to loosen a bolt.

Change 1 letter.

w r e n c h

★ **7. A miserable or despicable person.**

Take away 1 letter, then add 2.

w r e t c h

6. The _____ rode on her broomstick.

Change 1 letter.

w i t c h

★ **5. A crank or handle of a revolving machine.**

Change 1 letter.

w i n c h

4. A small amount. I added a ___ of salt to the recipe.

Take away the last letter, then add 2.

Multiple meaning word: to squeeze between two fingers.

p i n c h

3. In bowling, you want to knock all the ___ over.

Change 1 letter.

p i n s

2. Containers in which you store things.

Take away 2 letters, then add 1.

Have students list synonyms for *bin* (*basket, box, bucket*).

b i n s

1. Subtraction symbol: ____ sign.

Take away the first and last letters, then add 2.

m i n u s

Start Here

a m i n o

An _____ **amino** _____ **acid** _____ is an organic molecule and a building block of protein.

Read each clue and write the answer in the blanks.
Use the first and last words to fill in the sentence under the ladder.

HINT! Words with a ★ are more challenging!

SCIENCE

DON'T BE NERVOUS!

9. What you think with.
Add 1 letter.

_ _ _ _ _

8. Pieces of grain husk separated from flour after milling, used in cereal and bread. ★
Take away 2 letters, then add 1 letter.

_ _ _ _

7. Courageous.
Add 1 letter.

_ _ _ _ _

6. A praising review.
Take away 1 letter.

_ _ _ _

5. A black bird. ★
Take away 1 letter, then add 2.

_ _ _ _ _

4. A level surface.
Change 1 letter, then rearrange the letters.

_ _ _ _

3. Vessel that brings blood to the heart.
Change the last 2 letters.

_ _ _ _

2. To turn suddenly. ★
Take away 1 letter, then rearrange the letters.

_ _ _ _

1. A part of our body that allows us to feel sensations.
Take away 3 letters, then add 1.

Start Here

_ _ _ _ _

n e r v o u s

Your _____ system is made up of your _____ and nerve cells and fibers that transmit nerve impulses between parts of your body.

DON'T BE NERVOUS!
Answer Key and Teaching Notes

9. What you think with.

Add 1 letter.

b r a i n

8. Pieces of grain husk separated from flour after milling, used in cereal and bread. ★

Take away 2 letters, then add 1 letter.

Figure of speech: *mill around*, to wander aimlessly.

b r a n

7. Courageous.

Add 1 letter.

In pairs, have students repeat and complete, "A time I was really brave was when…"

b r a v e

6. A praising review.

Take away 1 letter.

r a v e

5. A black bird. ★

Take away 1 letter, then add 2.

r a v e n

4. A level surface.

Change 1 letter, then rearrange the letters.

Multiple meaning word: the opposite of *odd*.

e v e n

3. Vessel that brings blood to the heart.

Change the last 2 letters.

v e i n

2. To turn suddenly. ★

Take away 1 letter, then rearrange the letters.

v e e r

1. A part of our body that allows us to feel sensations.

Take away 3 letters, then add 1.

Start Here

n e r v e

n e r v o u s

Your __nervous__ system is made up of your __brain__ and nerve cells and fibers that transmit nerve impulses between parts of your body.

Name _____

Read each clue and write the answer in the blanks.
Use the first and last words to fill in the sentence under the ladder.

HINT! Words with a ⭐ are more challenging!

SCIENCE

PUMPING IRON

11. Liquid pumped by your heart.
Change 1 letter.

_ _ _ _ _

⭐ 9. A machine used to weave fabric.
Change 1 letter.

_ _ _ _ _

7. A place to swim.
Change 1 letter, then rearrange.

_ _ _ _

⭐ 5. A freshwater fish; rhymes with #4.
Change 1 letter.

_ _ _ _

⭐ 3. Parasitic insects that live in the hair of mammals.
Change 1 letter.

_ _ _ _

1. A round shape with no sides.
Take away 3 letters.

Start Here

10. When a flower opens up and is at its prettiest, it is in ____.
Add 1 letter.

_ _ _ _ _ _

8. A curve that bends around and crosses itself.
Rearrange the letters.

_ _ _ _

6. A long slender rounded piece of metal or wood.
Change 2 letters.

_ _ _ _

4. To approve of something.
Change 1 letter.

_ _ _ _

2. A small white grain.
Take away 2 letters, then rearrange the remaining letters.

_ _ _ _ _ _ _

c i r c u l a t e

The pumping of your heart allows your _____ to _____ throughout your body.

PUMPING IRON
Answer Key and Teaching Notes

b l o o d

b l o o m

l o o m

l o o p

p o o l

p o l e

p i k e

l i k e

l i c e

r i c e

c i r c l e

c i r c u l a t e

Start Here

11. Liquid pumped by your heart.
Change 1 letter.

★ **9. A machine used to weave fabric.**
Change 1 letter.
Show students a digital image of a loom.

7. A place to swim.
Change 1 letter, then rearrange.

★ **5. A freshwater fish; rhymes with #4.**
Change 1 letter.
Multiple meaning word: a weapon similar to a spear.

★ **3. Parasitic insects that live in the hair of mammals.**
Change 1 letter.

1. A round shape with no sides.
Take away 3 letters.

10. When a flower opens up and is at its prettiest, it is in ___.
Add 1 letter.

8. A curve that bends around and crosses itself.
Rearrange the letters.

6. A long slender rounded piece of metal or wood.
Change 2 letters.
Multiple meaning word: the northern and southern ends of a celestial object.

4. To approve of something.
Change 1 letter.

2. A small white grain.
Take away 2 letters, then rearrange the remaining letters.

The pumping of your heart allows your __blood__ to __circulate__ throughout your body.

Name _____

Read each clue and write the answer in the blanks.
Use the first and last words to fill in the sentence under the ladder.

SCIENCE

YUMMY!

11. To break down food in your body.
Add 2 letters.

— — — — — —

9. Two people singing together.
Add 1 letter.

— — — — —

7. A hint or suggestion.
Take away 1 letter.

— — —

5. Clean, with nothing added.
Change 1 letter.

— — — —

3. To make excessively dry. ★
Change 1 letter.

— — — — —

1. A tool to light a fire.
Take away 2 letters and rearrange. ★

— — — — —

Start Here

10. I have a very healthy ____ of fruits and vegetables.
Change 1 letter.

— — — — —

8. A payment that is required.
Change 1 letter.

— — — —

6. To heal of an illness.
Change 1 letter.

— — — —

4. To remove the outer layer. ★
Take away 2 letters, then add 1.

— — — —

2. The month after February.
Change 1 letter.

— — — — —

s t o m a c h

Your _____ is the organ that works to _____ your food.

174

TIP! You may want to offer students some extra support for these more challenging words, marked with a ⊛.

YUMMY!
Answer Key and Teaching Notes

11. To break down food in your body.
Add 2 letters.

9. Two people singing together.
Add 1 letter.

7. A hint or suggestion.
Take away 1 letter.
Multiple meaning word: a stick used in the game of pool to hit a ball. Show students a digital image of a pool cue.

5. Clean, with nothing added.
Change 1 letter.

⊛ **3. To make excessively dry.**
Change 1 letter.

⊛ **1. An tool to light a fire.**
Take away 2 letters and rearrange.

Start Here

d i g e s t

d i e t

d u e t

d u e

c u e

c u r e

p u r e

p a r e

p a r c h

M a r c h

m a t c h

s t o m a c h

10. I have a very healthy ____ of fruits and vegetables.
Change 1 letter.

8. A payment that is required.
Change 1 letter.
Homophone: *do*, any action.

6. To heal of an illness.
Change 1 letter.

⊛ **4. To remove the outer layer.**
Take away 2 letters, then add 1.
Homophone: *pair*, two of something.

2. The month after February.
Change 1 letter.

Your __stomach__ is the organ that works to __digest__ your food.

Name _____

Read each clue and write the answer in the blanks.
Use the first and last words to fill in the sentence under the ladder.

HINT! Words with a ★ are more challenging!

TECHNOLOGY

PULL THE LEVER!

11. A type of simple machine.
Change the first 2 letters.

9. A narrow passage between buildings.
Take away the first letter, then add 2.

★ **7. To fix something.**
Change 1 letter.

5. Someone who allows someone to borrow money.
Change 1 letter.

3. A kind of wall or border you put around the outside of a yard.
Change 3 letters.

1. Opposite of *always*.
Change 1 letter.

Start Here

10. A flat area between hills or mountains.
Add 1 letter.

8. An indoor shopping center.
Change the last 3 letters.

6. To loan something to someone.
Take away 2 letters.

★ **4. The front or back part of a car mounted over the wheels.**
Change 1 letter, then add 1.

2. If you have a high temperature, you have a ____.
Change 1 letter.

l e v e r

Both simple machines, a _____ has a grooved wheel, while a _____ is a bar with a balance point called a fulcrum.

PULL THE LEVER!
Answer Key and Teaching Notes

p u l l e y

v a l l e y

a l l e y

m a l l

m e n d

l e n d

l e n d e r

f e n d e r

f e n c e

f e v e r

n e v e r

l e v e r

11. A type of simple machine.
Change the first 2 letters.

9. A narrow passage between buildings.
Take away the first letter, then add 2.

⊛
7. To fix something.
Change 1 letter.

5. Someone who allows someone to borrow money.
Change 1 letter.
Point out that someone who borrows money is the *borrower*.

3. A kind of wall or border you put around the outside of a yard.
Change 3 letters.

1. Opposite of *always*.
Change 1 letter.

Start Here

10. A flat area between hills or mountains.
Add 1 letter.

8. An indoor shopping center.
Change the last 3 letters.

6. To loan something to someone.
Take away 2 letters.
Review tenses of this word (past: *lent;* present: *lend;* future: *will lend*).

⊛
4. The front or back part of a car mounted over the wheels.
Change 1 letter, then add 1.

2. If you have a high temperature, you have a _____.
Change 1 letter.
In pairs, have students share, "One time I had a fever, and I felt…"

Both simple machines, a _____ pulley _____ has a grooved wheel, while a _____ lever _____ is a bar with a balance point called a fulcrum.

Name _____

Read each clue and write the answer in the blanks.
Use the first and last words to fill in the sentence under the ladder.

WHAT TO WARE?

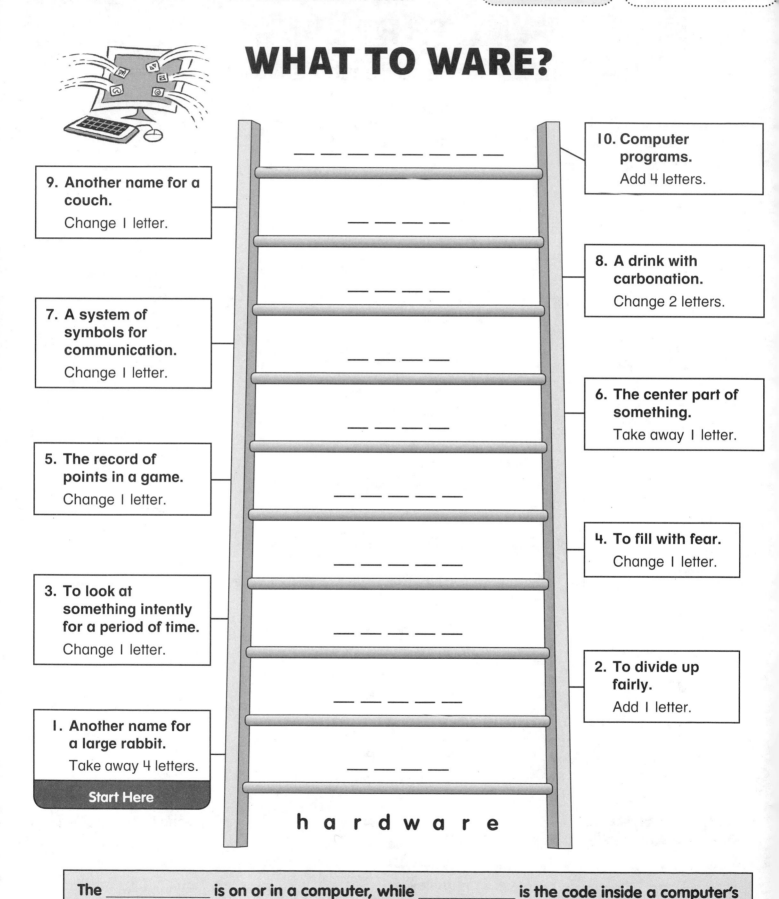

9. Another name for a couch.
Change 1 letter.

7. A system of symbols for communication.
Change 1 letter.

5. The record of points in a game.
Change 1 letter.

3. To look at something intently for a period of time.
Change 1 letter.

1. Another name for a large rabbit.
Take away 4 letters.

Start Here

10. Computer programs.
Add 4 letters.

8. A drink with carbonation.
Change 2 letters.

6. The center part of something.
Take away 1 letter.

4. To fill with fear.
Change 1 letter.

2. To divide up fairly.
Add 1 letter.

h a r d w a r e

The _____ is on or in a computer, while _____ is the code inside a computer's hard drive.

WHAT TO WARE?
Answer Key and Teaching Notes

s o f t w a r e

10. Computer programs.
Add 4 letters.

9. Another name for a couch.
Change 1 letter.

s o f a

s o d a

8. A drink with carbonation.
Change 2 letters.

7. A system of symbols for communication.
Change 1 letter.
Discuss how people use codes to communicate with each other.

c o d e

c o r e

6. The center part of something.
Take away 1 letter.

5. The record of points in a game.
Change 1 letter.

s c o r e

s c a r e

4. To fill with fear.
Change 1 letter.
Have students list synonyms for *scare* (*panic, alarm, shock, fright, terror*).

3. To look at something intently for a period of time.
Change 1 letter.

s t a r e

s h a r e

2. To divide up fairly.
Add 1 letter.

1. Another name for a large rabbit.
Take away 4 letters.
Homophone: *hair*, what grows from your scalp.

Start Here

h a r e

h a r d w a r e

The ____hardware____ is on or in a computer, while ____software____ is the code inside a computer's hard drive.

Read each clue and write the answer in the blanks.
Use the first and last words to fill in the sentence under the ladder.

ZEROES AND ONES

11. A computer that can travel with you.
Add 2 letters, then rearrange.

— — — — — — —

10. The sound of something dropping into water.
Add 1 letter.

— — — —

9. Another name for a fizzy sweet drink also called *soda*.
Take away 2 letters, then add 1.

— — —

8. The sound a baby chick would make.
Take away 2 letters, then add 1.

— — — —

⭐
7. A digital sound made to cover an offensive word.
Change 1 letter.

— — — — — —

6. To lose blood from the body.
Add 1 letter.

— — — — — —

5. Past tense of *bleed*.
Change 2 letters.

— — — —

4. Past tense of *speed*.
Take away 1 letter.

— — — —

3. Past tense of *spy*.
Take away 1 letter, then rearrange the letters.

— — — — — —

⭐
2. The positive aspects of something. Opposite of *downside*.
Take away 1 letter, then rearrange the letters.

— — — — — — —

⭐
1. An argument.
Take away the first 3 and last letters, then add 3.

Start Here

— — — — — — —

c o m p u t e r

One type of portable _____ is called a _____ ; it can be used in many places.

TIP! You may want to offer students some extra support for these more challenging words, marked with a ⭐.

ZEROES AND ONES
Answer Key and Teaching Notes

11. A computer that can travel with you.

Add 2 letters, then rearrange.

9. Another name for a fizzy sweet drink also called _soda_.

Take away 2 letters, then add 1.

Teach students that _pop_ is a palindrome, a word that is spelled the same forward and backward.

⭐ **7. A digital sound made to cover an offensive word.**

Change 1 letter.

5. Past tense of _bleed_.

Change 2 letters.

3. Past tense of _spy_.

Take away the 1 letter, then rearrange the letters.

⭐ **1. An argument.**

Take away first 3 and last letters, then add 3.

Start Here

l a p t o p

p l o p

p o p

p e e p

b l e e p

b l e e d

b l e d

s p e d

s p i e d

u p s i d e

d i s p u t e

c o m p u t e r

10. The sound of something dropping into water.

Add 1 letter.

8. The sound a baby chick would make.

Take away 2 letters, then add 1.

Multiple meaning word: to look through a small opening.

6. To lose blood from the body.

Add 1 letter.

Figure of speech: _my heart bleeds for you_, someone who feels really sorry for someone else.

4. Past tense of _speed_.

Take away 1 letter.

⭐ **2. The positive aspects of something. Opposite of _downside_.**

Take away 1 letter, then rearrange the letters.

One type of portable ___computer___ is called a ___laptop___; it can be used in many places.

Name _____

Read each clue and write the answer in the blanks.
Use the first and last words to fill in the sentence under the ladder.

TECHNOLOGY

KEY TO SUCCESS

11. Monopoly is a _____ game.
Add 1 letter.

_ _ _ _ _ _

9. A sound a dog might make when agitated.
Change 1 letter.

_ _ _ _ _

★ **10. A person who recites poetry.**
Change 1 letter.

_ _ _ _

8. To hesitate or refuse to do something.
Change 2 letters.

7. Another name for a dollar.
Change 1 letter.

_ _ _ _

6. A type of pickle.
Take away 1 letter, then add 2.

_ _ _ _

★ **5. A loud, confused noise.**
Change 1 letter.

_ _ _ _

4. A shelter for a lion or other animal.
Change 1 letter.

_ _ _

3. A female bird.
Take away the first letter, then change 1.

_ _ _

★ **2. The watery part of milk after the formation of curds.**
Add 1 letter.

_ _ _ _

1. Something to say to get someone's attention.
Change 1 letter.

_ _ _

Start Here

k e y

You use a _____ to type letters, numbers, or symbols into your computer.
(Hint! Make a compound word with the top and bottom words.)

KEY TO SUCCESS
Answer Key and Teaching Notes

11. Monopoly is a _____ game.
Add 1 letter.

9. A sound a dog might make when agitated.
Change 1 letter.

7. Another name for a dollar.
Change 1 letter.
Multiple meaning word: a proposal for a new law.

⊛ **5. A loud, confused noise.**
Change 1 letter.

3. A female bird.
Take away the first letter, then change 1.
Figure of speech: *mad as a wet hen*, to be really upset.

1. Something to say to get someone's attention.
Change 1 letter.

Start Here

b o a r d

b a r d

b a r k

b a l k

b i l l

d i l l

d i n

d e n

h e n

w h e y

h e y

k e y

⊛ **10. A person who recites poetry.**
Change 1 letter.

8. To hesitate or refuse to do something.
Change 2 letters.

6. A type of pickle.
Take away 1 letter, then add 2.

4. A shelter for a lion or other animal.
Change 1 letter.

⊛ **2. The watery part of milk after the formation of curds.**
Add 1 letter.
Homophone: *way*, a certain direction or path to be taken.

You use a __keyboard__ to type letters, numbers, or symbols into your computer.
(Hint! Make a compound word with the top and bottom words.)

Name _____

Read each clue and write the answer in the blanks.
Use the first and last words to fill in the sentence under the ladder.

AT YOUR FINGERTIPS

11. To press or select.
Change 1 letter.

_ _ _ _ _

10. An object that tells time.
Change 2 letters.

_ _ _ _ _

9. The feeling after a surprising or upsetting event.
Change 2 letters.

_ _ _ _ _

8. A pile of something one on top of another.
Take away the last letter, then add 2.

_ _ _ _ _

7. To pierce, often with a knife.
Take away 1 letter, then rearrange the letters.

_ _ _ _

6. To brag about something, often oneself. ★
Change 1 letter.

_ _ _ _ _

5. The land next to the ocean.
Add 1 letter.

_ _ _ _ _

4. How much you have to pay for something.
Change 1 letter.

_ _ _ _

3. A person who has guests.
Change 1 letter.

_ _ _ _

2. A flexible tube to transfer liquids.
Take away 1 letter.

_ _ _ _ _

1. A building in which people live.
Change 1 letter.

_ _ _ _ _

Start Here

m o u s e

To navigate on a computer and learn more about a topic online, use a _____ or touchpad to _____ on links you trust.

AT YOUR FINGERTIPS
Answer Key and Teaching Notes

11. To press or select.
Change 1 letter.

c l i c k

9. The feeling after a surprising or upsetting event.
Change 2 letters.

c l o c k

7. To pierce, often with a knife.
Take away 1 letter, then rearrange the letters.

s h o c k

s t a c k

5. The land next to the ocean.
Add 1 letter.
Multiple meaning word: to ride with little effort.

s t a b

b o a s t

3. A person who has guests.
Change 1 letter.

c o a s t

c o s t

1. A building in which people live.
Change 1 letter.
Multiple meaning word: the act of giving shelter.

Start Here

h o s t

h o s e

h o u s e

m o u s e

10. An object that tells time.
Change 2 letters.
Multiple meaning word: slang for hitting something.

8. A pile of something one on top of another.
Take away the last letter, then add 2.

6. To brag about something, often oneself.
Change 1 letter.

4. How much you have to pay for something.
Change 1 letter.

2. A flexible tube to transfer liquids.
Take away 1 letter.

To navigate on a computer and learn more about a topic online, use a _____mouse_____ or touchpad to _____click_____ on links you trust.

Name _____

Read each clue and write the answer in the blanks.
Use the first and last words to fill in the sentence under the ladder.

TECHNOLOGY

WORLDWIDE

11. **Silk material spun by spiders.**
    Change 1 letter.

★ 9. **Moisture on grass in the morning.**
    Take away 1 letter, then rearrange the remaining letters.

★ 7. **To walk into water.**
    Add 1 letter.

5. **Some streets only go one ___ for cars.**
    Change 1 letter.

3. **Opposite of peace.**
    Take away 1 letter.

1. **Putting letters together can make a ___.**
    Take away 1 letter.

Start Here

— — —

— — —

— — —

— — — —

— — — —

— — —

— — —

— — —

— — — —

— — — —

w o r l d

10. **To be married or joined together.**
    Rearrange the letters.

8. **Opposite of narrow.**
    Change 1 letter.

6. **A small mass of something.**
    Change 1 letter.

4. **What a dog does with its tail.**
    Change 1 letter.

★ 2. **A division of people or an area in a city for organizational purposes.**
    Change 1 letter.

When using the internet, the letters *www* stand for _____ wide _____.

WORLDWIDE
Answer Key and Teaching Notes

11. Silk material spun by spiders.

Change 1 letter.

Figure of speech: a *tangled web*, a confusing situation, often formed from deception.

w e b

w e d

10. To be married or joined together.

Rearrange the letters.

d e w

8. Opposite of *narrow*.

Change 1 letter.

w i d e

★ **9. Moisture on grass in the morning.**

Take away 1 letter, then rearrange the remaining letters.

w a d e

★ **7. To walk into water.**

Add 1 letter.

w a d

6. A small mass of something.

Change 1 letter.

5. Some streets only go one ___ for cars.

Change 1 letter.

w a y

4. What a dog does with its tail.

Change 1 letter.

w a g

3. Opposite of *peace*.

Take away 1 letter.

w a r

★ **2. A division of people or an area in a city for organizational purposes.**

Change 1 letter.

Multiple meaning word: A hospital room for many patients.

w a r d

1. Putting letters together can make a ___.

Take away 1 letter.

Start Here

w o r d

w o r l d

When using the Internet, the letters *www* stand for __world__ wide __web__.

Name _____

Read each clue and write the answer in the blanks.
Use the first and last words to fill in the sentence under the ladder.

TECHNOLOGY

LOADING TIMES

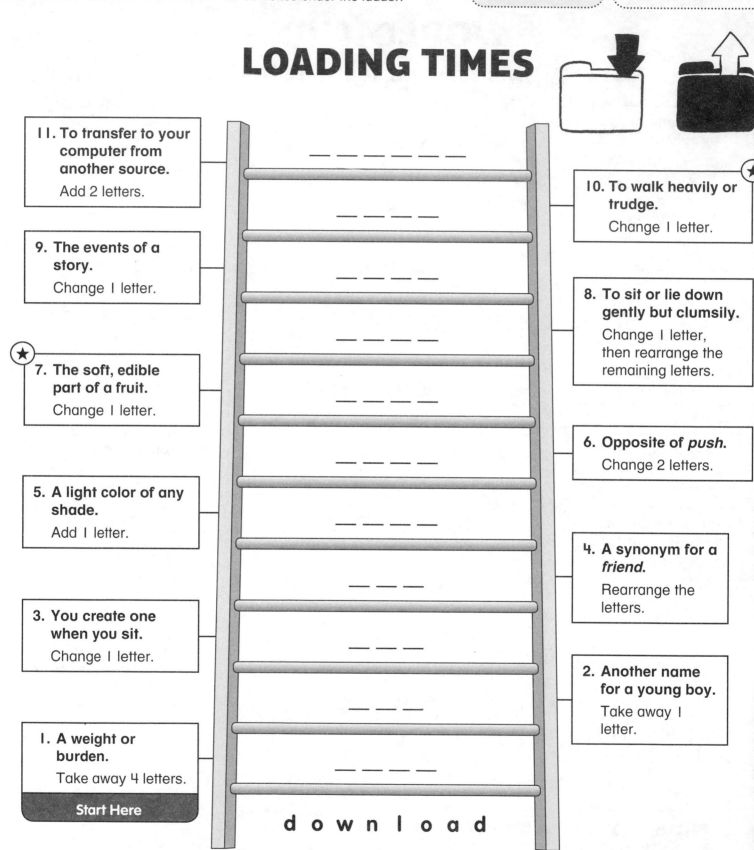

11. To transfer to your computer from another source.

Add 2 letters.

9. The events of a story.

Change 1 letter.

⭐ **7.** The soft, edible part of a fruit.

Change 1 letter.

5. A light color of any shade.

Add 1 letter.

3. You create one when you sit.

Change 1 letter.

1. A weight or burden.

Take away 4 letters.

Start Here

⭐ **10.** To walk heavily or trudge.

Change 1 letter.

8. To sit or lie down gently but clumsily.

Change 1 letter, then rearrange the remaining letters.

6. Opposite of *push*.

Change 2 letters.

4. A synonym for a *friend*.

Rearrange the letters.

2. Another name for a young boy.

Take away 1 letter.

d o w n l o a d

To transfer information from another source to your own computer is a _____, but transferring information from your computer to another source is an _____.

LOADING TIMES
Answer Key and Teaching Notes

11. To transfer to your computer from another source.
Add 2 letters.

u p l o a d

★ **10. To walk heavily or trudge.**
Change 1 letter.

p l o d

9. The events of a story.
Change 1 letter.
Multiple meaning word: to secretly plan something.

p l o t

8. To sit or lie down gently but clumsily.
Change 1 letter, then rearrange the remaining letters.

p l o p

★ **7. The soft, edible part of a fruit.**
Change 1 letter.

p u l p

6. Opposite of *push.*
Change 2 letters.

p u l l

5. A light color of any shade.
Add 1 letter.
Homophone: *pail,* a kind of bucket.

p a l e

4. A synonym for a *friend.*
Rearrange the letters.
Have students list synonyms for *pal* (*buddy, companion, chum*).

p a l

3. You create one when you sit.
Change 1 letter.

l a p

2. Another name for a young boy.
Take away 1 letter.

l a d

1. A weight or burden.
Take away 4 letters.

Start Here

l o a d

d o w n l o a d

To transfer information from another source to your own computer is a ___download___, but transferring information from your computer to another source is an ___upload___.

CLIMB A WORD LADDER!

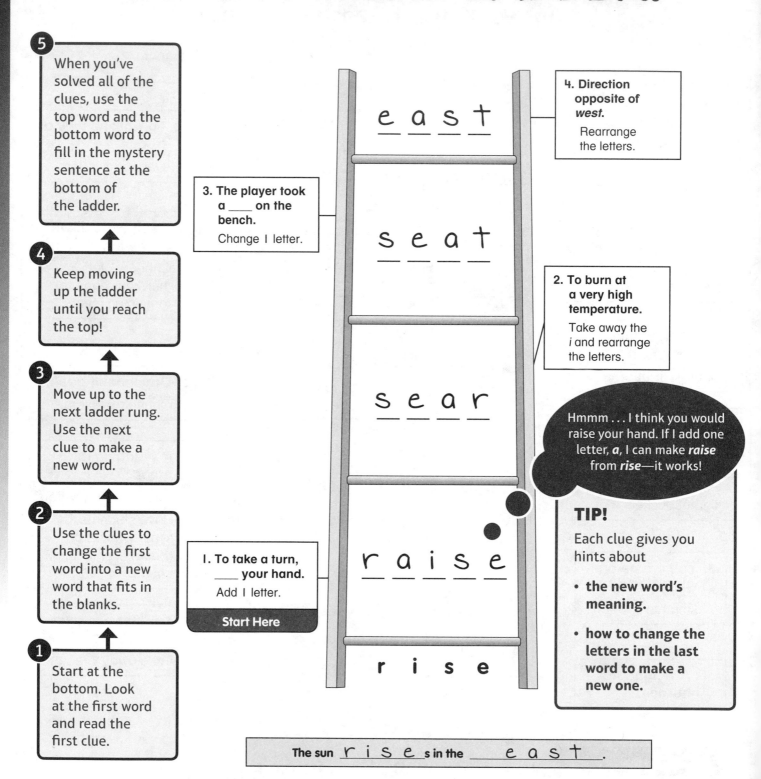

5 When you've solved all of the clues, use the top word and the bottom word to fill in the mystery sentence at the bottom of the ladder.

4 Keep moving up the ladder until you reach the top!

3 Move up to the next ladder rung. Use the next clue to make a new word.

2 Use the clues to change the first word into a new word that fits in the blanks.

1 Start at the bottom. Look at the first word and read the first clue.

e a s t

4. Direction opposite of *west*.
Rearrange the letters.

3. The player took a ____ on the bench.
Change 1 letter.

s e a t

2. To burn at a very high temperature.
Take away the *i* and rearrange the letters.

s e a r

Hmmm . . . I think you would raise your hand. If I add one letter, *a*, I can make *raise* from *rise*—it works!

TIP!
Each clue gives you hints about

- **the new word's meaning.**

- **how to change the letters in the last word to make a new one.**

1. To take a turn, ____ your hand.
Add 1 letter.

Start Here

r a i s e

r i s e

The sun r i s e s in the ____ e a s t ____.

Congratulations! You know how to solve the word ladder!

190

BUILD YOUR OWN LADDER!

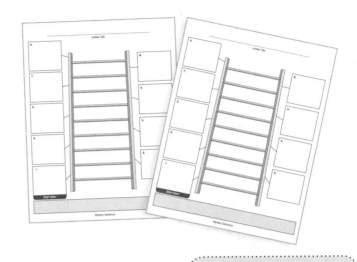

Materials

Use **two copies** of a blank word ladder template (page 193 or online).

- **Copy 1**: This is your answer key!

- **Copy 2:** This copy is for your friends to solve!

Directions

1. Choose two related words that aren't too long. Examples:

   - *big-large* (synonyms)

   - *sum-add* (topics you're studying)

   - *field-day* (events/news)

2. On Copy 1, write one word at the top of your ladder and one word at the bottom of your ladder.

3. List all the words in between, changing, adding, or taking away a letter or two at a time with each new word. These are the answers to your ladder!

> **HINT:**
>
> *It may be helpful to first make your list of words on a piece of scratch paper.*

> **TIP!**
>
> *Underline each letter in the answers to help you write the letter clues in the next step!*

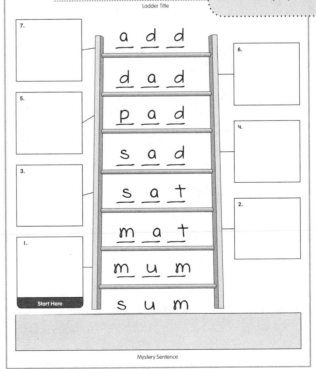

Copy 1

191

4. Write two clues about each new word. In the clue box, include

- a meaning clue.

- a letter clue (how to change the structure of the word).

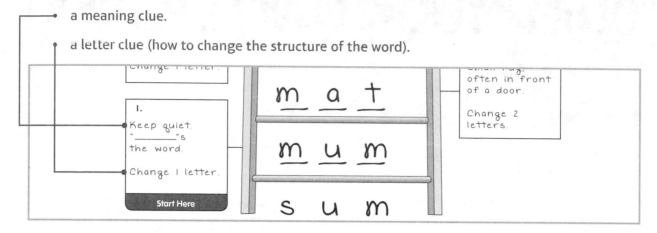

5. Write a Mystery Sentence at the bottom of the ladder that uses both words in a meaningful way.

You ___add___ to find the ___sum___ or total of a set of numbers.

Mystery Sentence

6. When your ladder is complete, use Copy 2 to

- fill in the first (bottom) word and all the clue boxes.

- add the Mystery Sentence at the bottom, leaving blank lines where the top and bottom words fit.

- add the exact number of lines in each rung for the letters in each word.

- add a relevant title.

7. Make copies of your Copy 2 page so that classmates, friends, family members, or teachers can try to solve your puzzle. Then use your original word ladder (Copy 1) to check their answers!

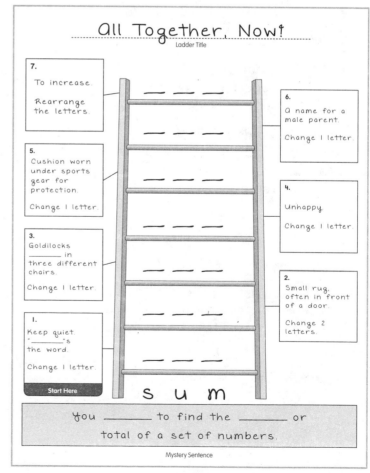

Copy 2